Routledge Revivals

The Poetry of Cercamon and Jaufre Rudel

The Poetry of Cercamon and Jaufre Rudel

Edited and Translated by
George Wolf and
Roy Rosenstein

Volume 5
Series A

First published in 1983 by Garland Publishing, Inc.

This edition first published in 2018 by Routledge
2 Park Square, Milton Park, Abingdon, Oxon, OX14 4RN
and by Routledge
52 Vanderbilt Avenue, New York, NY 10017, USA

Routledge is an imprint of the Taylor & Francis Group, an informa business

© 1983 by George Wolf and Roy Rosenstein

All rights reserved. No part of this book may be reprinted or reproduced or utilised in any form or by any electronic, mechanical, or other means, now known or hereafter invented, including photocopying and recording, or in any information storage or retrieval system, without permission in writing from the publishers.

Publisher's Note
The publisher has gone to great lengths to ensure the quality of this reprint but points out that some imperfections in the original copies may be apparent.

Disclaimer
The publisher has made every effort to trace copyright holders and welcomes correspondence from those they have been unable to contact.

A Library of Congress record exists under ISBN:

ISBN 13: 978-0-367-14032-8 (hbk)
ISBN 13: 978-0-367-14035-9 (pbk)
ISBN 13: 978-0-429-02984-4 (ebk)

The Garland Library
of Medieval Literature

General Editor
James J. Wilhelm, Rutgers University

Literary Advisors
Ingeborg Glier, Yale University
Thomas R. Hart, University of Oregon
Guy Mermier, University of Michigan
Lowry Nelson, Jr., Yale University
Aldo Scaglione, University of North Carolina

Art Advisor
Elizabeth Parker McLachlan, Rutgers University

Music Advisor
Hendrik van der Werf, Eastman School of Music

Ist trobador, entre ver e mentir (8.19). The pipe of a minstrel, viol at his side, excites a devil, who has his hands on a young girl. A capital of the nave at Vezelay, illustrating "profane music." (Courtesy of A. Allemand)

The Poetry of Cercamon and Jaufre Rudel

edited and translated by
GEORGE WOLF and ROY ROSENSTEIN

Volume 5
Series A
GARLAND LIBRARY OF MEDIEVAL LITERATURE

Garland Publishing, Inc.
New York & London
1983

© 1983 George Wolf and Roy Rosenstein
All rights reserved

Library of Congress Cataloging in Publication Data
Cercamon, 12th cent.
　Cercamon and Jaufré Rudel.
　(Garland library of medieval literature ; v. 5. Series A)
　1. Provençal poetry. 2. Provençal poetry—Translations into English. 3. English literature—Translations from Provençal. 4. Troubadours. I. Rudel, Jaufré. II. Title. III. Series: Garland library of medieval literature ; v. 5.
PC3365.E3C47　1983　　　849'.12'09　　　80-8959
ISBN 0-8240-9443-3

Printed on acid-free, 250-year-life paper
Manufactured in the United States of America

This book
is inscribed to
M. CHARLES ROSTAING
to whom the editors
are grateful for their introduction
to Old Provençal

Illumination heading the poems of Cercamon in Manuscript I, B.N. fr. 854, fol. 133r. Here the poet is stylized as an itinerant. (Courtesy of the Bibliothèque Nationale)

Preface of the General Editor

The Garland Library of Medieval Literature was established to make available to the general reader modern translations of texts in editions that conform to the highest academic standards. All of the translations are original, and were created especially for this series. The translations attempt to render the foreign works in a natural idiom that remains faithful to the originals.

The Library is divided into two sections: Series A, texts and translations; and Series B, translations alone. Those volumes containing texts have been prepared after consultation of the major previous editions and manuscripts. The aim in the editing has been to offer a reliable text with a minimum of editorial intervention. Significant variants accompany the original, and important problems are discussed in the textual notes. Volumes without texts contain translations based on the most scholarly texts available, which have been updated in terms of recent scholarship.

Most volumes contain Introductions with the following features: (1) a biography of the author or a discussion of the problem of authorship, with any pertinent historical or legendary information; (2) an objective discussion of the literary style of the original, emphasizing any individual features; (3) a consideration of sources for the work and its influence; and (4) a statement of the editorial policy for each edition and translation. There is also a Select Bibliography, which emphasizes recent criticism on the works. Critical writings are often accompanied by brief descriptions of their importance. Selective glossaries, indices, and footnotes are included where appropriate.

The Library covers a broad range of linguistic areas, including all of the major European languages with the exception of Middle English. All of the important literary forms and genres are considered, sometimes in anthologies or selections.

The General Editor hopes that these volumes will bring the general reader a closer awareness of a richly diversified area that has for too long been closed to everyone except those with precise academic training, an area that is well worth study and reflection.

James J. Wilhelm
Rutgers University

Contents

I. The Poetry of Cercamon

Introduction	3
Select Bibliography	23
Poetry	31
Textual Notes	63
Manuscripts	65
Glossary of Special Words	77
Index of Names	79
Index of Opening Lines	81
Manuscript a, pages 364–70	83

II. The Poetry of Jaufre Rudel

Introduction	95
Select Bibliography	111
Poetry	125
Textual Notes	151
Manuscripts	153
Glossary of Special Words	169
Index of Names	171
Index of Opening Lines	173
The Music of Jaufre Rudel by *Hendrik van der Werf*	175

The Poetry of Cercamon

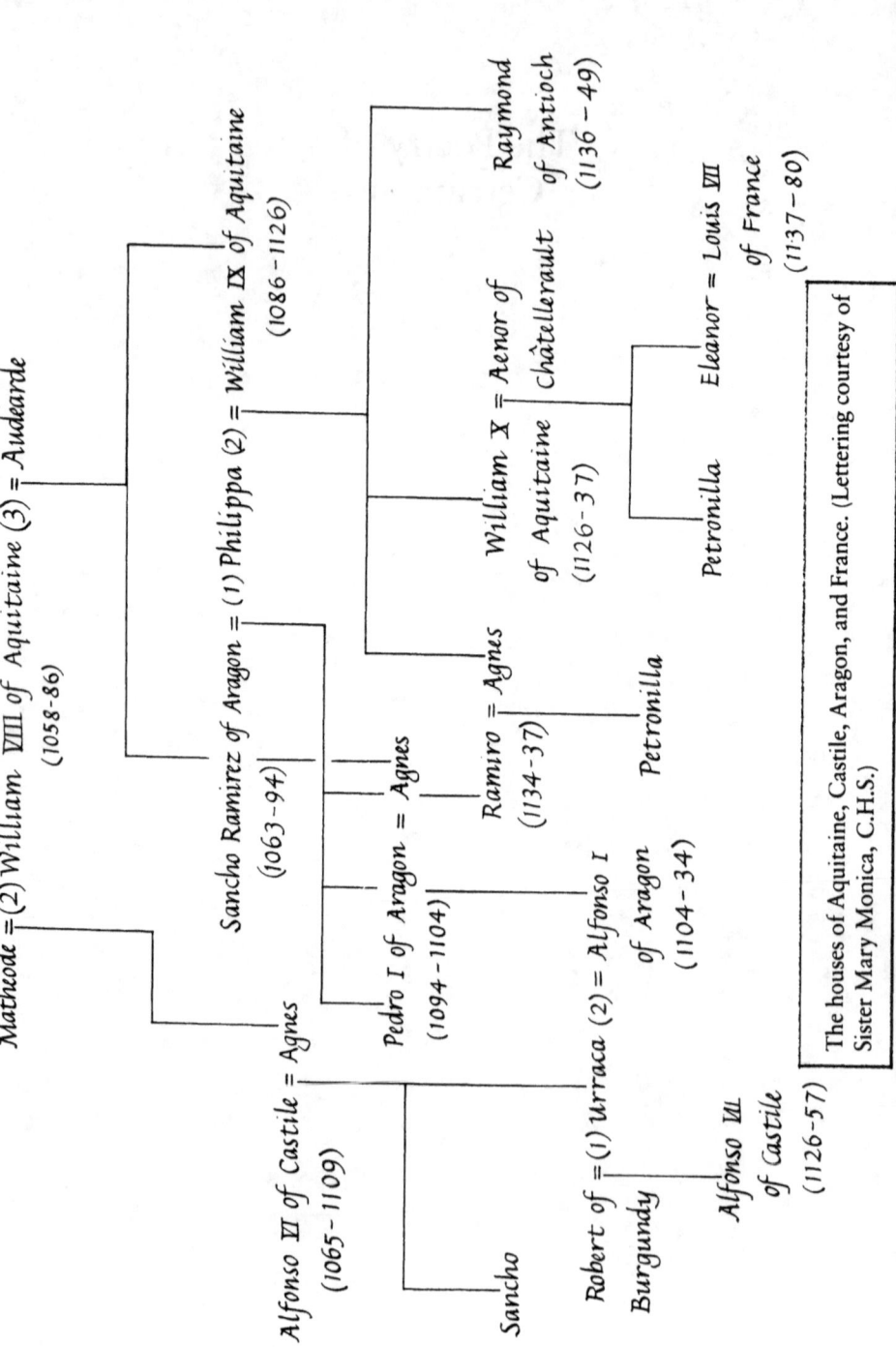

The houses of Aquitaine, Castile, Aragon, and France. (Lettering courtesy of Sister Mary Monica, C.H.S.)

Introduction

Life of the Author

Cercamon was a Southern French poet—Gascon, according to his biography—who wrote songs in Old Provençal during the second quarter of the twelfth century. One of these is a lament (No. 1) on the death of Duke William X of Aquitaine (Count VIII of Poitiers), son of William IX (VII of Poitiers), the troubadour. At the end of this lament Cercamon identifies himself. Since William X died on April 9, 1137, we may place the composition of this song in the spring or early summer of that same year.

Roughly the same date may be assigned to Poem 2, which is attributed to Cercamon in Manuscript R, the only manuscript to contain it. This poem is a debate between the poet and his companion, Guilhalmi, who tries to keep the poet from feeling sad because he has no patron, because the clergy will not help him in this situation, and because of the general decline of joy and amusement in the world. Guilhalmi tells the "master" that he will be well outfitted when "the Count of Poitiers comes." Later, he tells the poet that great good will come to him "from France," and further on that they will have "a new count at Whitsun." If this song is correctly ascribed, Guilhalmi's references are to Louis VII of France, who came south in the spring or early summer of 1137, after the death of William X, to marry William's daughter, Eleanor of Aquitaine. By doing this Louis became the eleventh Duke of Aquitaine.

Cercamon no doubt lost a patron in William X of Aquitaine, for after William's death the poet apparently had to find new lodgings. It is likely that Cercamon had Ebles II of Ventadorn in mind as a patron when he sent his lament to Ebles. Ebles is documented as having been a friend and younger contemporary of William IX of Aquitaine, as well as William's rival in high living and hospitality. Known to Latin chroniclers as "The Singer," he seems to have presided over a lively court which sponsored poets. Not only Cercamon, but Marcabru, Bernart Marti, and Bernart de Ventadorn mention Ebles's "song school." Bernart de Ventadorn, who sang at Ebles's court, implies in one of his songs (*Lo temps vai e ven e vire*) that he is sad that he may not be good enough for the "school of Ebles" (line 23). Bernart Marti, in a frank love song (*Quan l'erb' es reverdezida*), says in the envoi that he is sending his song to Ebles because in the latter "the love between a knight and a lady is enjoyed." Marcabru, on the other hand, inveighs against false love, and attacks Ebles directly in one of his songs (*L'iverns vai e·l temps s'aizina*), accusing him of "maintaining foolishness over reason" (lines 73–76). It seems likely that Marcabru, and possibly others, regarded Ebles's court as too libertine for their tastes. We do not know what Cercamon's attitude to Ebles was, and it is not known if Cercamon went to Ventadorn and followed the "school" there.

Cercamon may also have looked toward Spain after William X's death. In Poem 1, he says that "youth is downcast" because of the loss of the Count; now it can find no lodging, "except with Alfonso, who has won joy over." This is probably Alfonso VII of Castile rather than Alphonse-Jourdain of Toulouse. The relations between Toulouse and Aquitaine had not been cordial during the early twelfth century, since William VII of Poitiers had twice attempted to take over the rival county. There were, however, close ties between Aquitaine and Spain (see genealogical chart), which may suggest that Cercamon went to Spain and stayed at the court of Alfonso VII of Castile. In any event, Alfonso was known to be a patron of poets, as can be seen in the mention of his generosity by the troubadours Marcabru and Alegret.

The biographical remarks just stated have been inferred from Cercamon's poems. The only medieval testimony to the poet is the brief *vida* (biography) found in the thirteenth-century Italian manuscripts I and K (text of I):

> Cercamon was a minstrel from Gascony, and wrote songs and pastorals in the old style. And he searched the whole world, [or] as much of it as he could, and for this he was called Cercamon (Search-the-World).
>
> Cercamons si fo uns joglars de Gascoingna, e trobet vers e pastoretas a la uzansa antiga. E cerquet tot lo mon lai on el poc anar, e per so fez se dire Cercamons.

Introduction

There is also a mention of Cercamon in the biography of Marcabru in Manuscript A:

> Afterwards, he [Marcabru] stayed so long with a troubadour named Cercamon that he began to write songs.
>
> Apres estet tant ab un trobador que avia nom Cercamon qu'el comensset a trobar.

How much fiction or fact there is in these biographies has been much debated in troubadour studies. It is not difficult to see how the biographer could have invented an explanation for the name *Cercamon*. However, it is not clear why, if he did, he should have invented Gascony as Cercamon's homeland, beyond the fact that Cercamon mentions the Gascons twice in Poem 1; for the poet also mentions the Burgundians, the Normans, the French, the Limousins, the Angoumois, the people of Aunis, the Spanish, and the Aragonese. Instead, it is possible that the biographer based at least part of his *vida* on what was generally known about this early poet; thus Cercamon's Gascon origin may have a basis in fact.

Cercamon's Poem 8 links him with the Second Crusade. In stanza 8 the poet exhorts worthy people to depart for Edessa, which had been part of the Byzantine Empire since 1031 and fell to the Moslems in 1144. Louis VII, chosen by Pope Eugenius III to organize the Crusade, set out for the East with his wife Eleanor and his army in June 1147.

Rita Lejeune believes that Poem 7 was also written at this time, in the Holy Land, and that it alludes to the scandal of Eleanor of Aquitaine. Eleanor and Louis had a falling out upon their arrival in Antioch in March of 1148. Her uncle Raymond, brother of William X of Aquitaine, was Prince of Antioch, and Eleanor's favorable attitude to Raymond's advice that Louis should join him in attacking Aleppo resulted in Louis's jealousy, and rumors of an affair between Eleanor and her uncle. Three allusions in Poem 7 lead Lejeune to conclude that the song was written in the context of this situation. The first is the poet's mention of his beloved as being far away: he wants *Saint Salvador* to give him lodging "there in the land where my lady stays." It sounds as if this means that she is in France. Second, he chides the lady "who sleeps with two or three," who is "worthless from now on," and whose sin "will be gossiped of as far as Poitou." According to Lejeune, this could be Eleanor. Third, the poet asks the messenger to tell his beloved that, if he misses their appointed meeting, he will be dead, "by St. Nicholas." Since St. Nicholas was the patron saint of sailors, this may well mean that Cercamon was planning on sailing home to France.

Should Lejeune's theory be correct, it would nicely complete Cercamon's biography, since we have no more evidence for his existence after 1147–48. It is not unlikely that he should have gone from William X's court to that of Louis VII and that he should have followed Louis and Eleanor on Crusade. At this point we can only speculate. The song itself gives no firm proof.

We have placed Cercamon's love songs, none of which is datable, somewhat arbitrarily between Poem 1 and Poems 7 and 8. About ten years separate Poem 1 from Poem 8, and both of these songs deal with similar themes. If the love songs are placed correctly between, it is possible that Cercamon spent time at the court of Ventadorn, changed his style accordingly, and returned with even greater fervor to his preaching style after leaving the "school of Ebles." But this is sheer speculation, and the love songs might be placed anywhere.

One more item of biographical relevance should be discussed. In Poem 8 Cercamon appears to associate himself with *soudadiers*. These were men under wage for either military or entertainment purposes (possibly both). He says that he is concerned because the *soudadier* can find no one to house him, thanks to the cunning advisors of stingy nobles. That Cercamon himself was a trained professional—a type of *soudadier*—is suggested by the fact that he is called *maïstre* by his companion Guilhalmi in Poem 2. The term *maïstre* would have applied to an individual trained, for example, in musical composition, who may originally have been connected to the church or monastery. In any event, Cercamon then attacks *trobadors*, who "between truth and lying, confound lovers and husbands and wives, and say that love is devious." He calls them "these false *sirven*" (8.25). In feudal society, a *sirven* designated a "servant," often of intermediate status, generally endowed by the lord with a minor position of administration, jurisdiction, or command. The term *sirven* or *sergent* did not, however, always strictly mean a soldier or an administrator. Marc Bloch describes them as "a whole small world of men-servants, of workers attached to the workshops of the court, of officers who helped govern men or the household" (p. 468). Thus, a *sirven* was for Cercamon probably close in rank and function to a *soudadier*. And, as suggested above, it is natural to envisage Cercamon himself as a *soudadier* or *sirven*. If so, then in attacking *trobadors*, Cercamon is attacking *sirvens* like himself, but *sirvens* who have gone wrong, and hence who are false. Cercamon, then, places himself on the side of the *soudadiers* and *sirvens*, and against *trobadors*, who sow discord by encouraging wanton behavior (see the Vezelay capital in the frontispiece). It is worth recalling that it was for encouraging "foolishness" (i.e. false love) that Marcabru reproached Ebles of Ventadorn. However, it is purely hypothetical whether Cercamon and Marcabru, in mentioning the bad influence of *trobadors*, were alluding to the "school of Lord Ebles."

In sum, it is against this social background that we should see Cercamon, who assumed the role of the *sirven* in at least some of his poems, and who, in addition to singing of love, exhorted youth to follow excellence and distinction, castigated nobles for stinginess and for their libertine morality, and attacked the deception and infidelity which undermined true love.

Artistic Achievement

Cercamon's biography says that he composed *vers* and pastoral poems in the antique or old style (see Faral in Select Bibliography). We shall see about the *vers*; we have no pastoral poems from him, although we do have two pastorals by Cercamon's alleged pupil, Marcabru, and these are the first known pastorals in a modern language. Both poets also give us the first known example of the *tenso* or debate poem. Cercamon has left three love poems; but in this genre he was preceded by William IX/VII. Cercamon is also credited with the first *planh*, or lament, in a modern language.

Although love songs, laments, and debates as genres of Latin literature preceded Cercamon and Marcabru by centuries, these poets have a unique connection with a type of poem peculiar to their era, the *sirventes*. A *sirventes* is traditionally defined as a troubadour poem dealing with a non-amorous subject. Bertran de Born is the most famous of the writers of *sirventes*, although with him the term means "war poem" almost exclusively. The meaning "war poem" may have derived from an earlier usage of the Provençal word: one might assume that the term *sirventes* was connected somehow to a *sirven*; yet exactly what the connection is has never been clear. Bearing in mind the role of the *sirven* as discussed above, it is likely that *sirventes*, an adjective become noun, meant in effect "a poem by a sergeant." Cercamon and Marcabru, being *sirvens* of a kind, produced these sergeant's poems, which exhort, castigate, or encourage men, and specifically youth, to worthy deeds. Probably *sirventes* originally meant "a harangue," and came with Bertran de Born to designate a military harangue in particular, taking the inspiration from some of Marcabru's poems which include military exhortation. But the earlier usage was broader, including moral as well as military themes.

The general question about the nomenclature of Cercamon's songs is a delicate one. At the end of Poem 1, Cercamon says that the lament (*lo plaingz*) is well constructed. At the beginning of Poem 4 he says that he wishes to begin a new song (*un novel chant*). At the beginning of Poem 6 he says that his song (*chanz*) has not been heard afar; but at the end he says that the song is plain: *plas es lo vers*. Should we therefore label the songs *Plaingz, Chanz, Vers*? The question of whether *vers*, for example, is a full-fledged poetic genre has been discussed by J.H. Marshall, who argues that before 1150 *vers* designated a courtly song in general. It is uncertain whether Cercamon would have placed the title *Vers* above some or all of his songs had he seen them untitled in a *chansonnier*. It is perhaps best to leave *plaingz, chanz,* and *vers* as common, rather than proper, nouns.

Cercamon's real poetic achievement lies in the songs themselves, and one is struck immediately by their variety in so restricted a number. Jeanroy has referred to the "archaic character" of Cercamon's poems, especially in their versification. The poems are composed of between six and nine full stanzas; most stanzas contain six or seven lines, while Poem 2 contains nine lines per stanza. There are fairly few rhymes, and most are masculine (final-syllable stressed). Most of Cercamon's lines contain seven or eight syllables, and Poem 7 contains an internal rhyme. This is comparatively uncomplicated versification, which, as Jeanroy points out, is characteristic of the earliest troubadours.

Several of Cercamon's themes are as unique as his versification. His lament (No. 1), as mentioned, brings in moralizing themes as well as those of mourning; not only has Count William VIII's death caused sadness but it has hastened the demise of joy and youth and the rise of worthlessness. All good virtues have died with him. Cercamon makes many topical references, giving valuable historical testimony as well as a fascinating glimpse into an otherwise little-known poetic milieu.

Cercamon's debate poem (No. 2) is a kind of companion piece to his lament. It gives interesting historical evidence from the point of view of a professional poet in 1137. In the dramatic dialogue between the poor poet and his companion there is a brief picture of one aspect of life at that time.

The love songs are valuable because they give us early examples of a genre that achieved great fame in the hands of later poets. *Quant la douch'aura* (No. 3) portrays a timid lover, fearing rejection but hoping for acceptance, who captures his situation in the phrase "I am cautious and rejoice." In *Ab lo temps* (No. 4) the lover is crushed by a separation from his lady caused by hateful slanderers. The poet indulges in effusive praise and description of the lady's beauty and goodness, includes a general reflection on love, and ends in a moving appeal, conveyed through the messenger, for acceptance.

Per fin'amor (No. 5) is somewhat more playful. In it the poet again appeals for the lady's love but with greater hope and humor. He says that he would abandon lords and ladies to go into her service, and that, if accepted, he would wage war on his neighbors, as well as perform other remarkable things. But she is hard to win, and he would hardly have sought her love if he had known how difficult it would be to obtain it. *Assatz es ora* (No. 6) seems to lift love onto a higher plane and in this respect is reminiscent of Jaufre Rudel. There is consistent ambiguity here between a love in flesh and blood and one that, "thanks to God and St. John," seems more permanent. Yet we are never completely free of the possible fleshly references in *leis*, which can be either the lady, or love itself, *amor*, a feminine noun in Old Provençal.

The satiric poems are among the most singular in troubadour poetry, and are to be classified with the songs of Marcabru, to which they are similar. *Ab lo pascor* (No. 7), for several reasons, has been much discussed. As a whole, it may be taken both as a love song and as a satire on deceit in love. It begins on a bright note in spring, then plunges into sadness. The poet cannot enjoy the season because the worthless are as successful in love as the best people; youth and high deeds are in decline, while worthlessness has taken hold in love affairs. Cercamon blames womanizing husbands, false lovers, and specifically the loose lady (whom Rita Lejeune takes to be Eleanor of Aquitaine). After this lengthy tirade, Cercamon asks for lodging in his own lady's land, where he hopes that she at least will keep the promise she made to him.

Pus nostre temps (No. 8) develops the same themes. As the gloom of winter settles on the world, we must rejoice in love. Cercamon gives an eloquent praise of love, which is here definitely spiritual yet has its own temporal rewards of joy and distinction. The poet then attacks the enemies of true love: troubadours who lead people astray into the ways of lust; and stingy nobles and their advisers, who shut their doors to the poor mercenary poet. But Cercamon grows tired of thinking about them, and returns to the love which fills him with joy. He ends the poem with a call to the Crusade; all worthy people should depart for Edessa and abandon the perilous world.

These satiric poems are perhaps Cercamon's most remarkable. In their dual theme they resemble Romanesque tympana, with Christ on one side flanked by a vision of Heaven and beatitude, facing a vision of Hell and damnation. Cercamon portrays the damnation of false love and all who perpetrate it; in contrast he offers the beatitude of true love and its rewards.

A poet who was a kind of popular preacher, Cercamon embodies the directness and simplicity of early troubadour lyric, as well as its most powerful themes which, in all likelihood, he had a hand in creating.

Sources and Influences

In the wake of the eleventh-century revival of the classics, the themes of Latin poetry enjoyed a new vogue, especially in France. Eleventh and twelfth-century Latin poetry attests to the new fashion in love poetry and in satire. Poets learned not only from Ovid, but from noted contemporaries such as Hildebert of Lavardin. Following the example of noted ecclesiastic poets, young men who came to the cathedral schools wrote a great deal in imitation of classical poetry, employing the schoolroom techniques of their own day. Their

Introduction

knowledge of verse composition was formed by Ovidian elegies, by rhetorical treatises, and by liturgical music. Many of these men, either unable or unwilling to further their ecclesiastical status, returned to society to seek their fortunes with rich patrons, if possible. They contributed to an overpopulation of educated versifiers too numerous to be accommodated in their chosen profession. With this situation in mind, it is not surprising to find some classical themes, for example from Ovid, filtering into verse as remote from the schools as was troubadour poetry.

There are several themes reminiscent of Ovid in Cercamon's poems, to give one example of a literary source. Among passages which reflect Ovidian themes is Poem 3.9–12, where Cercamon expresses his desire for what he cannot have. This recalls Ovid's line in *Amores* 2.19.3: *quod licet, ingratum est; quod non licet, acrius urit* (What is lawful is unwanted; what is not allowed more bitterly burns). The lover's sickly state (Nos. 3.25 ff., 4.34) is described in *Ars Amatoria* 1.729–38. The common theme of the flatterer separating the lover from his lady (No. 4.10–11) is found in the form of the old hag Dipsas in *Amores* 1.8, who spends an entire poem counseling the lady. The messenger (No. 4.43) appears in *Amores* 1.11.7. Cercamon in Poem 5, stanza 7, speaks of the feats and sacrifices promised by the lover if the lady gives him her love; this is a central theme of *Ars Amatoria*, book 1. Cercamon alludes to the theme that everything must capitulate to love, and he could have found this in *Ars Amatoria* 1.269 ff. The lover as captive (No. 3.5, 47) is a frequent Ovidian theme (*Amores* 1.2.27, 30, etc.), as is the lover as servant (No. 3.29; *Amores* 1.3.5). The lover is at war with love in *Ars Amatoria* 1.21–22, *Amores* 1.9 passim, 2.9.1–8; he finds himself in a similar situation in Cercamon's Poem 3.5–8.

In satire, several influences converged to form the unique product of the moralizing poems of the early troubadours. The classical satirists, Juvenal and Persius, worked their influence indirectly through clerical poets. Preachers—popular, clerical, and monastic—also had a definite impact upon poets of a moralizing bent. The Bible provided the framework for the preachers; its language is reflected in many literary forms of the twelfth century. Cercamon's praise of love, for example, is colored by the language of passages such as *Wisdom* 8.7:

> One cannot serve this love so much

> That its reward will not redouble a thousand times;
> For distinction and joy and everything, and more,
> Those who are capable of it shall have.
> (Cercamon, 8.7–10)

> If a man love justice, her labors have great virtues;
> for she teaches temperance and prudence and justice and fortitude,
> which are such things as man can have nothing more profitable in life . . .
> (*Wisdom*, 8.7)

Comparison of the above-mentioned passages will give some idea of the kind of influence the various forms of Latin culture enjoyed among the early troubadours. Classical, clerical, and monastic themes were popular among poets of the time, who found these themes in their own learning and handed them on to other poets in their poems.

That vernacular poets influenced each other is evident from the dissemination of general themes, and, in a more focused way, from the idiom, vocabulary, and commonplaces of the poetic language. The first vernacular poet whose influence we can trace among the troubadours is William IX of Aquitaine, Count VII of Poitiers. For example, in the domain of vocabulary, the notion of deference finds form in the word *aclis*, which both William IX and Cercamon use in their poems: William (7.25–27) says that no one will be true to love if he is not deferential toward it; Cercamon (5.3) says that he will always be deferential toward love. William says that he would not exchange (*camjar*) one of his "horses" for gold or silver (1.18). Cercamon mentions his being "exchanged," or "crossed" (*cambiatz*), by a fickle woman (6.15). "To chide," in the sense of "to give counsel," is conveyed in William by *castiar* (2.10) and the noun (*mos*) *casteis*; *castiar* means the more usual "to correct" in Cercamon (8.37).

Joven, "youth," is a word which occurs in both William and Cercamon. It implies high spirits in William (1.3, 4.3), but in Cercamon it implies, perhaps in addition to high spirits, an inherent worthiness and is linked with the word *pretz*, not found in William. The unusual *lati* occurs in both poets, meaning "Latin" only once in William (11.24), where it is opposed to *romans*; otherwise it means "language," possibly connoting "idiom," or even "dialect." One of

Introduction

the ladies William meets on horseback addressed him in her *lati* (5.19); and each of the birds speaks in its own *lati* (W. 10.3; C. 3.3). In William, *malvatz* applies to men who boast about their deeds but who do not perform any (3.6) and is the opposite of *lo melhor* (6.14); in Cercamon it is linked with the adjectives *enojos* and *savai* (7.9) and so has a stronger sense than in William's poems. In both poets *malvestatz* is the opposite of *proeza* (W. 2.15; C. 8.30; see also C. 7.12) and implies worthlessness or degeneracy. The word *pechat* is used for a humorous purpose in William (5.7): the lady who refuses to love a loyal knight commits "a great mortal sin." In Cercamon the *pechat* is adultery (7.28).

In view of their mention of or connection with the Second Crusade, one of the most interesting verbal parallels between Cercamon and Jaufre Rudel is the appearance in both of the theme of "lodging." Jaufre's use is famous (6.16–17), the "distant lodging"; Cercamon wishes to "be put up" in his lady's land (7.43). Important to both poets is the theme of an *amistatz*, a love affair (C. 7.13; J. 5.8). Both poets refer to love "behind curtains" (C. 4.49; J. 4.13). Both are "concerned" or "anxious" (*cossiros soi*, C. 3.49; *suy cossiros*, J. 5.15) because they have no assurance of acceptance by their ladies. Neither poet is "able to guess about the future" with respect to the love of his lady, and Jaufre is uncertain how he will be able to go to see his distant love (*de s'amor no suy devis*, C. 3.33; *no·n sui devis*, J. 6.27).

Two sets of passages are particularly interesting in raising the question of influence. The first concerns an idiomatic formula:

Dieu en lau e Sanh Jolia (W. 6.29)	era·n *lau Dieu et* Saint Joan
I praise God and St. Julian for it	(C. 6.16)
	now I praise God and St. John for it

e *laus en lieys e Dieu e* lor (J.R. 2.25)
and I praise her and God and them for it

The second concerns a minor theme, the "(foolish) burden":

ar non puesc plus soffrir *lo fais* (W. 11.31)	et ab aitan pot si liurar *del fays* qu'assatz en fai trabucar e perir (C. 8.47–48)
now I can no longer endure the burden	and thus he can throw off the burden

> which makes many fall down and
> perish
>
> soi descargatz *de fol fais* (J.R. 2.56)
> I have cast off a senseless burden

The words most frequently found among all three poets are *joi* and *jauzir*, which reflect the poets' preoccupations with the theme of joy in its many aspects.

The affinity between Cercamon and Marcabru is familiar, but its nature has been debated. What is sure is that Marcabru's influence on later poets is more tangible than that of Cercamon. No one knows if Cercamon really was the master of Marcabru, as one of Marcabru's biographies states. However, an inventory of images shows that there are many fewer borrowings between Cercamon and Marcabru than there are between Marcabru and the later poets who followed the early satirists. The general themes common to Cercamon and Marcabru do not prove precedence in one direction or the other. These themes include "true love," "the decline of joy and youth," "the rise of worthlessness." Cercamon and Marcabru initiated these literary themes; the contemporaneity of the two poets is perhaps more important than the question of which came first.

Cercamon's love poems may be regarded as taking part in the fashion of the time. As was suggested in the Life of the Author, Cercamon may have written them with the patronage of Ebles of Ventadorn in mind; hence they may be direct precursors of the genre which was to be perfected by Bernart of Ventadorn and later poets. His lament is the first, and certainly not the last, of its kind. The same may be said of the debate, although the subject matter of this poem is unique. Finally, the moralizing satires, with those of Marcabru, are the first of their kind, and influenced a handful of Cercamon's younger contemporaries, such as Alegret, Bernart Marti, Peire of Auvergne, Bernart of Venzac, and Gavaudan. To the list may be added Guilhem Godi, whose one poem, *Si·l gen cours*, is very similar in structure to, and may have been influenced by, Cercamon's *Ab lo pascor* (No. 7). As for metrical influence, Istvan Frank's *Répertoire* reveals that the meter and rhyme-scheme (though not rhymes) of only three of Cercamon's poems were reproduced, and in all three cases by only one poet: No. 3 by Peire of Auvergne, No. 5 by Daude de Pradas, and No. 6 by Guilhem de Cervera.

Introduction

Moralizing satire was given new life in the thirteenth century by Peire Cardenal, who was no doubt familiar with the poetry of his noted predecessor Marcabru. Poets of the genre who followed Cardenal, e.g. Aymar de Rocafiza, Bernart Alanhan de Narbona, Bernart de la Barta, Guilhem Augier Novella, Peire de la Mula, Pons Barba, Raimon Gaucelm de Beziers, Uc de Murel, and others, molded the genre to their own purposes, but in so doing assured its continuity with the poems of the earliest troubadour satirists, perhaps the first of whom is Cercamon.

Editorial Policy for This Text and Translation

The aim of this edition of the poems of Cercamon is to use previous editions in conjunction with manuscripts as a basis for reassessing the texts. One result has been texts in which cruces and irregularities left as such by Jeanroy are resolved. We have emended or chosen variant readings where necessary, not always agreeing with Jeanroy. Where Jeanroy sometimes alters the graphy of the base manuscript, we have reproduced the graphies as they stand. Our choice of a base manuscript is primarily for graphic uniformity; but we have not been bound to the base when a variant reading has seemed to be clearly better.

This said, the problem of base manuscripts arises for only three of Cercamon's poems, and for one of those the choice is between only two manuscripts, the text of one of which is clearly superior. In the two more problematic cases, we differ from Jeanroy in one of them, No. 3, for which he chose C, and we choose L. In fact, Jeanroy used L's stanza order and many of L's readings in his text of the poem. As far as substantive readings are concerned, L is the best manuscript. Jeanroy preferred to print C's text only, as he says, "because of its Languedocian origin and because of the regularity of its orthography." The Textual Notes here indicate where Jeanroy strayed from the graphy of C in this poem and others and show where we differ from Jeanroy in substantive readings and emendations. Among differences of note are the solution of the crux *pareisa·l teit novel* at 2.47; this was left unsolved by Jeanroy.

The differences from Jeanroy in No. 3 are fairly numerous, and the Textual Notes should be consulted for these. In No. 7 we restore the internal rhyme, offer a solution in conformity with this rhyme in line 38, and provide a solution to the crux concerning the rhyme word *conqes* in line 48. As for differences in general from Jeanroy, ours is a more conservative approach in cases where an alternate reading or spelling does not make a great difference in meaning to the text. This includes cases of spelling, of morphology, and of formulaic phrases which are roughly equivalent in sense. However, quite often we have followed Jeanroy, and his edition remains valuable though it exhibits a tendency to normalize arbitrarily, while at the same time leaving some of the more difficult textual problems unsolved.

The choice of Cercamon's texts is fairly uncontroversial. In Poems 1, 3, and 8 Cercamon identifies himself as the author. Poem 2 exists only in Manuscript R, conforms to Cercamon's style, and is attributed to him by that manuscript. In the case of Poems 4 and 6, these are found only in Manuscript a, are attributed to him there, and again offer no reason, on the count of style, to deny Cercamon authorship. Poem 7 is also found only in a. This poem is quite close in theme and style to Poem 8 and so is probably correctly attributed. Jeanroy doubts the authenticity of Poem 5. It is attributed to Cercamon in Manuscript D, and is anonymous in f. We accept Cercamon's authorship here, and consider Jeanroy's argument against it invalid. That the poet presents himself as "a lord in a position to be generous and to wage war on his neighbors" is no doubt a literary pose and is, in any case, only one interpretation. It is likely that the poet means that if the lady gave him her love, then he would be so "exalted" that he would wage war on his neighbors, etc.; that is, her love will give him great but perhaps metaphoric powers. This passage would have even more effect for an audience who knew that Cercamon was a lowly-born professional poet and was thus striking an ironic pose. We agree with Jeanroy on stylistic grounds that P-C 112.2 is to be rejected.

In our metrical symbolism, we have departed from the usage of István Frank in transferring the prime mark (') from syllable-numbers to rhyme letters. We symbolize the number of syllables by Arabic numerals and rhyme-types by lower-case letters. The prime mark designates a feminine rhyme. *i* and *j*, *u* and *v* have been distinguished following modern convention.

We would like to thank Geneviève Brunel of the Institut de

Introduction

Recherche et d'Histoire des Textes in Paris for her untiring efforts to procure and send information and photographs of manuscripts. We are grateful to the librarians of the New York Public Library, the Vatican Library, the Estense Library in Modena, and the Bibliothèque Nationale in Paris for providing microfilms and photographs, and for permitting us to reproduce them in our pages.

Professors Margaret Switten and Gerald A. Bond have made helpful comments and suggestions on the texts and translations. Professor Hendrik van der Werf has kindly provided us with musical transcriptions and a musical introduction. We express our thanks to Mr. C.A. Robson, who gave in-depth guidance and assistance in the conception of the work and with texts of Cercamon. Maggy Wolf has spent many hours with this book; it has benefited from her criticism, from her accompaniment of the labors of one of the editors, and from her assistance with photography and production.

We are especially indebted to James J. Wilhelm for giving us the opportunity to be a part of this series and for guiding the work at every stage. It is thanks to his encouragement and his patience that the work was able to be completed.

New York   G.W.
Paris   R.R.

Modena, d'Este Library, R.4.4, fol. 196v (Italian hand, 13th century). Beginning in the second column, Manuscript D's version of *Per fin'amor m'esjauzira*. It is preceded by P-C 112.2, which is preceded by D's version of Poem 3. (Courtesy of the d'Este Library)

Modena, d'Este Library, R.4.4, fol. 197r. Ending at the top of the first column, Manuscript D's version of *per fin'amor m'esjauzira*. (Courtesy of the d'Este Library)

·Ġeŋʃlmō·

ar uey ſeınr a tot dıa lo ıoı el ʒeþoɾe e nom

ſoɾeɾ la eleɾɲa· non pueſe muʒaıɾ nom coſoɾt· co ſaɪv eı

conoıſ ſamoɾt· lo ſıgneſ que bɾav e cɾıaɪ· ꝛ enuıoıı ſon

ſoneɾ p foɾt· eaɾ lı coue ſeɱɾ ſa uıda· e plo noıa ꝛ ḿe
Maıſtre ſı dıeuſ me ualba lr dıreɪ ſo q coue· nıſ u aıı
ſo no uos calla· eaɾ lı elere no uos coue ſaɲ lɾ· eaɾ lo
uos remþs ue ſoner· q anreu a eal guaɾʒɪʃ· q uos dıu
pılaſtɾ o real q maıſ uos ualba· eaɾ lo coɱt ʒe prıneuſ
ue· Guılhalm nō prets meıll[fo] q oɲeſ p maſı
maıſ uoleɾıa una calla eſtreg rener e mo ſt· no faɾıa
polr· eſſteſ e aureıɪ ſɪɾuellı· cɪɾɾaeſ la loɾ mſe· eaɾ ſo
ſo euɲ lu daıllı· q ſare a laureuɪ mſe lɾ· Maıſtre gɾ
lemanſa poʒen auʒ ſı ſoſıeɪʒ· Guılhalmı noſtra u anaıɪ
nō eret ſı eqṁ uos me dıʒet· maıſtre eaɾ nom eɪeɾeɪ·ſ
lɾ uos uerɾa ʒe ſaınſa ſı areore lo uolet· guılhelm eal e
premſa yos ʒo dıeuſ eo uos muſten· Maıſtre n u
arı cozarʒe· ʒeſın m ʒoɱe leuger· guılhalm ſobre lo
guarge uos areɾɪıa uoloner· maıſte ınſ lo ʒeſtrer a
an lı oıne ʒe parırgeɾ p ſuſtener al rerrer· guılh eıu
ſteɾ e ſaluare Maıſtre ıoſ
la bıoſta uos partı al ʒeſt nouel· guılhalm lr par eŋ
uos coſta lo meuſ oſtalſ ʒel eaſtel· maıſtre coı̅ nou
aureɪ nos a parıeulla· quſ þıgaru lı̅ ꝛ bel· guılh ſı
es deueeſtoɲ· uos m þıgarıı daureuɪ boreel· ʒıııı e

Paris, Bibliothèque Nationale, français 22543, folio 48v. The only extant copy of Poem 2, in MS. R. (Courtesy of the Bibliothèque Nationale)

Rome, Vatican Library, Reg. Lat. 1725, fol. 75r. The French romance *Guillaume de Dôle*. At the bottom of the second column (line 1299) appears the first stanza of *Lanqan li jorn*. (Courtesy of the Vatican Library).

Select Bibliography

I. Major Editions and Transcriptions of Manuscripts

Bertoni, Giulio. "Rime provenzali inedite." *Studj di Filologia Romanza*, 8 (1901), 423–26. Text of 1, 4, 6, 7. (MS. a)

———. "Nuove rime provenzali." *Studi Romanzi*, 2 (1904), 78–79. Text of 8. (MS. a)

———. *Il Canzoniere provenzale di Bernart Amoros, Complemento Campori*, Fribourg, 1911, pp. 204–7. Text of 3; additional notes on previously printed texts. (MS. a)

Dejeanne, Jean-Marie L. "Le troubadour Cercamon." *Annales du Midi*, 17 (1905), 27–62. This edition, which includes all the texts given here, owes much to Jeanroy and is similar to Jeanroy's 1922 edition.

Grützmacher, L. "Fünfter Bericht an die Gesellschaft für das Studium der neueren Sprachen in Berlin über die in Italien befindlichen provenzalischen Liederhandschriften." *Archiv für das Studium der Neueren Sprachen und Literaturen*, 34 (1863), 435. Text of 3. (MS. L)

Jeanroy, Alfred. *Les Poésies de Cercamon*. CFMA 27. Paris: Champion, 1922. This has been the standard edition and includes all the texts given here.

Mahn, Carl A.F. *Gedichte der Troubadours in provenzalischer Sprache*. 4 vols. Berlin, 1856–73; rpt. Slatkine, III, 141. Text of 8. (MS. I)

———. "Der Troubadour Cercamon." *Jahrbuch für Romanische und Englische Literatur*, 1 (1859), 83–100. The first attempt at a critical edition; texts of 2, 3, P–C 112.2, 8.

Mussafia, Adolfo. "Del codice Estense di rime provenzali." *Sitzungsberichte der Königlichen Akademie der Wissenschaften zu Wien, Phil.-Hist. Klasse*, 55 (1867), 445–46. Text of 5. (MS. D)

Pakscher, A., and Cesare De Lollis. "Il canzoniere provenzale A (Cod. Vat. 5232)." *Studj di Filologia Romanza*, 3 (1891), 444–45. Text of 8. (MS. A)

Pelaez, Mario. "Il canzoniere provenzale L." *Studi Romanzi*, 16 (1921), 144. Text of 3. (MS. L)

Tortoreto, Valeria. *Il trovatore Cercamon*. Modena: S.T.E.M.-Mucchi, 1981. Appeared too late to be consulted.

II. *English Translations and Major Anthologies*

Appel, Carl. *Provenzalische Chrestomathie*. 6th ed. Leipzig, 1930; rpt. Olms, p. 53. Text of 3.

Audiau, Jean, and René Lavaud. *Nouvelle Anthologie des troubadours*. Paris: Delagrave, 1928, pp. 19–22. Text and trans. of 3.

Bartsch, Karl. *Chrestomathie provençale*. 6th ed. rev. E. Koschwitz. Marburg, 1904; rpt. AMS, cols. 51–54. Text of 5.

Blackburn, Paul. *Proensa: An Anthology of Troubadour Poetry*, intro. G. Economou. Berkeley: California, 1978, pp. 25–30. Trans. of 2, 4, 5.

Bonner, Anthony. *Songs of the Troubadours*. New York: Schocken, 1972, pp. 42–43. Trans. of 3.

Goldin, Frederick. *Lyrics of the Troubadours and Trouvères*. New York: Doubleday, 1973; rpt. Smith, pp. 96–99. Text and trans. of 3.

Hamlin, Frank R., Peter T. Ricketts, and John Hathaway. *Introduction à l'étude de l'ancien provençal*. Geneva: Droz, 1967, pp. 59–63. Text of vida, 8.

Hill, Raymond T., and Thomas G. Bergin. *Anthology of the Provençal Troubadours*. 2nd. ed., ed. Bergin et al. 2 vols. New Haven: Yale, 1973; I, 27–30. Texts of 1, 3.

Meyer, Paul. *Recueil d'anciens textes bas-latins, provençaux et français*, 1re partie. Paris, 1877, pp. 70–72. Text of 5.

Nelli, René, and René Lavaud. *Les Troubadours*. 2 vols. Bruges: Desclée de Brouwer, 1960, 1966; II, 38–42. Text and trans. of 3.

Pound, Ezra. *Translations*. Intro. Hugh Kenner. New York: New Directions, 1963, pp. 428–31. Trans. of 3.

Purcell, Sally. *Provençal Poems*. Oxford: Carcanet, 1969, pp. 24–25. Trans. of 3.

Riquer, Martin de. *Los Trovadores*. 3 vols. Barcelona: Editorial Planeta, 1975; I, 220–35. Texts and trans. of *vida*, 1, 3, 4, 8.

Rochegude, Henri de. *Le Parnasse occitanien*. Toulouse, 1817, p. 250. Text of 3.

Wilhelm, James J. *Medieval Song: An Anthology of Hymns and Lyrics*. New York: Dutton, 1971, pp. 118–20. Trans. of 3.

III. Critical Writings and Related Works

Adams, Edward L. *Word Formation in Provençal*. New York: Macmillan, 1913.

Angélique, Janine. *Le Troubadour Cercamon*. Mémoire de Licence à l'Université de Liège, 1970. Thorough treatment of various aspects of Cercamon studies.

Anglade, Joseph. *Grammaire de l'ancien provençal*. Paris: Klincksieck, 1922.

———. Review of Dejeanne. *Annales du midi*, 36 (1924), 320–22. Notes Jeanroy's omission of the "chansonnier de Sault."

Appel, Carl. "Tristan bei Cercamon?" *Zeitschrift für Romanische Philologie*, 41 (1921), 219–27. Argues that Cercamon mentions Tristan in 7.38.

Bertoni, Giulio. "Noterelle provenzali." *Revue des Langues Romanes*, 45 (1902), 348–52. Notes that the discovery of 1 in MS. a supports Rajna's conclusion about 2; confirms Mahn's attribution of 8 to Cercamon.

Bloch, Marc. *La Société féodale*. Paris: Albin Michel, 1939.

Brucker, Charles. "Pour une étude stylistique de l'adjectif dans la poésie lyrique d'oc et d'oil: Cercamon." *Mélanges Charles Camproux*. Montpellier, 1978, 57–70.

Brunel, Clovis. Review of Dejeanne. *Bibliothèque de l'Ecole des Chartes*, 84 (1923), 388. Brief favorable notice.

Camproux, Charles. "A propos d'une chanson pieuse." *Revue des Langues Romanes*, 77 (1965), 19–38. Detailed commentary on Jeanroy's text and trans. of 6; concludes that it is the beginning of *trobar clus*.

Cluzel, Irenée M. "Les plus anciens troubadours et la légende amoureuse de Tristan et Iseult." *Mélanges István Frank*. Saarbrucken, 1957, pp. 155–70. Argues in this and following articles in favor of Appel's view.

——. "Cercamon a connu Tristan." *Romania*, 80 (1959), 275–82.

——. Review of Delbouille (1959). *Cahiers de Civilisation Médiévale*, 3 (1960), 362.

Delbouille, Maurice. "Cercamon n'a pas connu Tristan." *Mélanges Angelo Monteverdi*. 2 vols. Modena, 1959; I, 198–206. Argues in this and following articles against Appel's view.

——. "Non, Cercamon n'a pas connu Tristan." *Romania*, 81 (1960), 409–25.

——. "Tristan dans la pièce *Ab lo pascor* de Cercamon." *Romania*, 87 (1966), 234–47. Responds to Lejeune's article of 1959.

De Lollis, Cesare. "Proposte di correzioni ed osservazioni ai testi provenzali del ms. Campori." *Studj di Filologia Romanza*, 9 (1902), 153–55. Comments on Bertoni's semi-diplomatic edition.

Dumitrescu, Maria. "L'*escola N'Eblon* et ses représentants." *Mélanges Rita Lejeune*, Gembloux, 1969; I, 107–18. Illuminating hypotheses on *trobadors* and the "school of Ebles."

Errante, Guido. *Marcabru e le fonti sacre dell'antica lirica romanza*. Florence: Sansoni, 1948. Adduces some Biblical passages which shed light on Cercamon's poems.

Faral, Edmond. "La pastourelle." *Romania*, 49 (1923), 241–42. Suggests that *a la uzansa antiga* in the *vida* means "in the manner of the ancients."

FEW: See Wartburg.

Frank, István. *Répertoire métrique de la poésie des troubadours*. Paris: Champion, 1953, 1957.

Gallais, Pierre. "Bléheri, la cour de Poitiers et la diffusion des récits arthuriens sur le continent." *Actes du VIIe Congrès National de Littérature Comparée*. Paris, 1967, 47–79. Suggests that Bleheri imported Breton matter to William IX's court; mentions Arthurian themes in troubadours.

Jeanroy, Alfred. "Sur la tençon *Car vei fenir a tot dia*." *Romania*, 19 (1890), 394–402. Agrees with Rajna (1877) against Zenker (1881).

———. Review of Zenker (1892). *Romania*, 22 (1893), 316–17. Acknowledgment of concessions by Zenker.

Kastner, Leon E. "Marcabrun and Cercamon." *Modern Language Review*, 26 (1931), 91–96. Argues that Cercamon could not have been the teacher of Marcabru.

Köhler, Erich. "Sens et fonction du terme *jeunesse* dans la poésie des troubadours." *Mélanges René Crozet*. Poitiers, 1966, pp. 569–83. Explains "youth" in terms of the rise of the petty knighthood.

———. "Die *Sirventes-Kanzone*: 'genre bâtard' oder legitime Gattung?" *Mélanges Rita Lejeune*. Gembloux, 1969; I, 159–83. Says that this genre reflects the situation vs. the aspirations of the petty knighthood.

Kolsen, Adolf. "Zu Appels Artikel über Cercamon, *Ab lo pascor*." *Zeitschrift für Romanische Philologie*, 41 (1921), 553–54. Agrees with Appel's reading *Tristan*, and emends *enqer* to *encor* in 7.38.

Lawner, Lynne. "Norman ni frances." *Cultura Neolatina*, 30 (1970), 223–32. Suggests that this phrase refers to the humanistic Latin poets of the Loire School.

Lejeune, Rita. "L'allusion à Tristan chez le troubadour Cercamon." *Romania*, 83 (1962), 183–209. Re-edits 7 and argues for Appel's view with Kolsen's emendation.

Levi, Ezio. "Due trovatori antichissimi nell'onomastica italiana del sec. XII: Marcabru e Cercamon." *Romania*, 55 (1929), 254–56. Adduces later evidence of persons called *Cercamundus* and *Marcabrunus* in Italy.

Levy, Emil. *Petit Dictionnaire provençal-francais*. Heidelberg: Winter, 1909. (PD)

———. *Provenzalisches Supplement-Wörterbuch*. 8 vols. Leipzig: Reisland, 1894–1924; rpt. Olms. (SW)

Marshall, John H. "Le *vers* au XIIe siècle: genre poétique?" *Revue de Langue et Littérature d'Oc*, 12–13 (1962–63), 55–63. Valuable reflections on the sense of the word *vers* at various periods of the 12th and 13th centuries: *vers* came to evoke the earliest troubadour period.

Meyer, Paul. Review of Bertoni (1902). *Romania*, 33 (1904), 299–300. Brief notice.

Mölk, Ulrich. *Trobar Clus—Trobar Leu*. Munich: Fink, 1968, 15–40. Comments on the relationship of Cercamon's poems to the origin of *trobar clus*.

Mouzat, Jean. "Quelques hypothèses sur les poèmes perdus d'Eble II, Vicomte de Ventadour." *Cultura Neolatina*, *18* (1958), 111–20. Attributes several poems to Ebles with debatable success.

Paris, Gaston. Review of Zenker (1899). *Romania*, *18* (1889), 629. Brief notice.

P-C: Pillet, Alfred, and Henry Carstens. *Bibliographie der Troubadours*. Halle, 1933; rpt. New York: Franklin, 1968.

Pillet, Alfred. "Beiträge zur Kritik der ältesten Trobadors." 89. *Jahresbericht der Schlesischen Gesellschaft für Vaterländische Cultur*. Breslau, 1911, 7–8. Comments on the internal rhyme of 7.

Pirot, François. *Recherches sur les connaissances littéraires des troubadours occitans et catalans des XIIe et XIIIe siècles: Les sirventes-ensenhamens de Guerau de Cabrera, Guiraut de Calanson, et Bertrand de Paris*. Memorias de la Real Academia de Buenas Letras de Barcelona, *14*. Barcelona, 1972. Sheds historical light on the earliest troubadour period.

Pollmann, Leo. *Die Liebe in der hochmittelalterlichen Literatur Frankreichs*. Frankfurt: Klostermann, 1966. Uses the love poems as evidence for characterizing the love ethic of the "school of Ebles."

Rajna, Pio. "Spigolature provenzali, I: Cercalmon, *Car vei fenir a tot dia*." *Romania*, *6* (1877), 115–19. First article to note correct date of 2.

Raynouard, François J.M. *Lexique roman*. 6 vols. Paris, 1836–44; rpt. Winter.

Rieger, Dietmar. *Gattungen und Gattungsbezeichnungen der Trobadorlyrik. Untersuchungen zum altprovenzalischen Sirventes*. Beihefte zur Zeitschrift für Romanische Philologie, *148*. Tubingen: Niemeyer, 1976. Theorizes on the constitution of a system of poetic genres among the troubadours.

Römer, Ludwig. *Die volkstümlichen Dichtungsarten der altprovenzalischen Lyrik. Excursus: Untersuchung über die Cercalmon zugeschriebenen Gedichte*. Ausgaben und Abhandlungen aus dem Gebiete der romanischen Philologie, *26*. Marburg, 1884. Discusses the attribution of Cercamon's poems, with stress on form; R. considers the poems relevant to his discussion of folk poetry.

Roncaglia, Aurelio. "Marcabruno, *Lo vers comens quan vei del fau*. 1: Marcabruno e Cercamondo." *Cultura Neolatina*, *11* (1951), 25–27. Presents previous scholars' arguments against Cercamon as teacher of Marcabru.

Scheludko, Dimitri. "Über die Theorien der Liebe bei den Trobadors: Cercamon." *Zeitschrift für Romanische Philologie*, 60 (1940), 213–20. Portrays Cercamon's conception of love as derived from William IX and Marcabru.

Spanke, Hans. *Untersuchungen über die Ursprünge des romanischen Minnesangs. Zweiter Teil: Marcabrustudien.* Abhandlungen der Gesellschaft der Wissenschaften zu Göttingen, Phil.-Hist. Klasse, Dritte Folge, 24. Göttingen, 1940. Contains valuable comments on the form of Cercamon's poems in relation to Marcabru and to liturgical music.

Stengel, Edmund. Review of Mahn (1859). *Jahrbuch für Romanische und Englische Literatur*, 12 (1871), 239–40. Further clarification of Mahn's misidentification of Raynouard's quotation.

Suchier, Walther. Review of Pillet (1911). *Zeitschrift für Romanische Philologie*, 36 (1912), 504–06. Brief notice.

Thiolier-Méjean, Suzanne. *Les Poésies satiriques et morales des troubadours du XIIe à la fin du XIIIe siècle.* Paris: Nizet, 1979. Thorough thematic treatment of troubadour satire.

Tobler, Adolf. "Nachtrag zu Mahn's Artikel über Cercamon." *Jahrbuch für Romanische und Englische Literatur*, 1 (1859), 212–14. Discovers Mahn's omission of 5, owing to a misidentification of a quotation of Raynouard.

———. Review of Jeanroy (1890). *Zeitschrift für Romanische Philologie*, 15 (1891), 276. Brief notice with suggested emendation of 2.

Tortoreto, Valeria. "Cercamon, maestro di Marcabru?" *Cultura Neolatina*, 36 (1976), 61–93. Adduces evidence in favor of the statement that Cercamon was the master of Marcabru.

Wartburg, Walther von. *Französisches etymologisches Wörterbuch.* 31 vols. Bonn, et al., 1922–date.

Zenker, Rudolf. "Zu Guilhem Ademar, Eble d'Uisel, und Cercamon." *Zeitschrift für Romanische Philologie*, 13 (1889), 294–300. Attempts to identify the *maïstre* in 2 with Raimon de Miraval instead of Cercamon.

———. "Zu Peire d'Alvernhes Satire und nochmals *Car vei fenir.*" *Zeitschrift für Romanische Philologie*, 16 (1892), 437–51. Defends his hypothesis against Jeanroy (1890) but makes some concessions.

Poetry

1. LO PLAING COMENZ IRADAMEN

1. Lo plaing comenz iradamen
    d'un vers don hai lo cor dolen;
    ir'e dolor e marrimen
    ai car vei abaissar Joven:
    Malvestatz puej'e Jois dissen 5
    despois muric lo Peitavis.

2. Remazut son li prez e·il lau
    qi solon issir de Peitau;
    ai! com lo plain[o] li Barrau;
    [p]e[za·m] s'a longa[s] sai estau; 10
    Segners, lo baro q'ieu mentau
    metet[z], si·us platz, em Paradis.

3. Del comte de Pitieu mi plaing
    q'era de Proeza compaing;
    despos Pretz et Donars soffraing, 15
    peza·m s'a lonjas sai remaing;
    Segners, d'efern lo faitz estraing,
    qe molt per fon genta· sa fis.

4. Glorios Dieus, a vos me clam,
    car mi toletz aqels q'ieu am; 20
    aissi com vos formetz Adam,
    lo defendetz del fel liam
    del foc d'efern, qe non l'aflam,
    q'aqest segles nos escharnis.

5. Aqest segle teing per enic 25
    qe·l paubre non aten ni.[·l] ric;
    ai! con s'en van tuit mei amic,

                    Lament

                       1.

1. In grief I begin the lament
    In a song which pains my heart;
    Grief and pain and chagrin
    I feel, for I see Youth debased:
    Baseness[1] is on the rise, and Joy is on the wane   5
    Since the Poitevin[2] has died.

2. They are no more, the rewards and praises
    Which used to come from Poitou;
    Ah! how the Barrau[3] lament him;
    It is a burden if I remain here longer;   10
    Lord, the baron whom I call to mind--
    Place him, if you please, in Paradise!

3. It is the Count of Poitiers I lament,
    Who was the companion of Excellence;
    Since Distinction and Generosity are lacking,   15
    It is a burden for me to remain here long;
    Lord, keep him far from Hell,
    For his end was most noble.

4. Lord of Glory, I appeal to you,
    For you take from me those whom I love;   20
    Just as you created Adam,
    Safeguard him from the cruel bond
    Of the fire of Hell, so that it will not burn him;
    For this world mocks us.

5. I consider this world despicable   25
    For it cares neither for rich nor poor;
    Ah! how all my friends pass away,

```
           e sai remanem tuit mendic;
           pero sai ben q'al ver afic
           seran li mal dels bos devis.                          30


     6.    Gasco cortes, nominatiu,
           perdut aves lo segnoriu;
           fer vos deu esser et esqiu,
           don Jovenz se clama chaitiu,
           qar un non troba on s'aiziu,                           35
           mas qan N'Anfos, q'a Joi conqis.


     7.    Plagnen lo Norman e Frances,
           e deu lo be plagner lo reis
           cui [el] laisset la terra e·l creis;
           pos [ai]tan grant honor li creis,                      40
           mal estara si non pareis
           chivaugan sobre Serrazis.


     8.    Aqil n'an joia, cui qe pes,
           de Limozi e d'Engolmes;
           si el visques ni Deu plagues,                          45
           el los agra dese conqes;
           estort en son car Dieus lo pres,
           e·l do[l]s n'es intratz en Aunis.


     9.    Lo plaingz es de bona razo,
           qe Cercamonz tramet N'Eblo;                            50
           ai! com lo plaigno li Gasco,
           cil d'E[s]paign' e [cil] d'Arago;
           Sant Jacme, membre·us del baro
           qe denant vos jai pelegris.
```

Rejected readings of a: 7. remazuc   26. paubres   29. vet
30. dals b.   33. Ser v.   35. us non t.   38. E dieu
42. Chivauge   43. A. van; pez   49. raggo   54. devant

And we poor beggars remain here;
   But I know that at the Last Judgment
   The bad shall be separated from the good.   30

6. Courtly and renowned Gascons,
   You have lost your lordship;
   It must be harsh and bitter for you,
   And for this Youth is miserable,
   Since it finds none it can find welcome with,   35
   Except Lord Alfonso,[4] who has gained Joy.

7. The Normans and the French[5] lament him,
   As indeed should the king[6]
   To whom he left his land and his offspring;
   Since his territory so greatly increases,   40
   He will be to blame if he doesn't appear,
   Riding against the Saracens.

8. Whoever may grieve for it, they are joyous,
   The men of the Limousin[7] and of the Angoumois;
   If he had lived and had it pleased God,   45
   He would have conquered them instantly;
   They are saved because God took him,
   And for this, mourning has begun[8] in Aunis.

9. The lament has a good subject
   Which Cercamon sends to Lord Ebles;[9]   50
   Ah! how the Gascons mourn him,
   As do the Spanish and Aragonese;
   St. James,[10] remember the baron
   Who lies as a pilgrim before you.

[1]See Textual Notes.
[2]William X of Aquitaine, who died April 9, 1137.
[3]See Textual Notes.
[4]Probably Alfonso VII of Castille, who reigned from 1126 to 1157; see Life of the Author. Possibly also Alphonse-Jourdain of Toulouse.
[5]See Textual Notes.
[6]Louis VI of France; see Textual Notes.
[7]See Textual Notes.

2. CAR VEI FENIR A TOT DIA

1. "Car vei fenir a tot dia
   [l'amor], lo joy, e·l deport,
   e no·m socor la clerzia,
   non puesc mudar no·m cofort
   co fay, can conois sa mort, 5
   lo signes, que bray e cria,
   e·n mou son sonet per fort,
   que·l cove fenir sa via,
   e plus no·i a de conort."

2. "Maïstre, si Dieus me valha, 10
   ben dizetz so que cove;
   mas ja d'aisso no vos calha
   car li clerc no vos fan be;
   car lo bos temps ve, so cre,
   que auretz aital guazalha 15
   que vos dara palafre,
   o renda que mais vos valha,
   car lo coms de Peitieus ve."

3. "Guilhalmi, non pretz mealha
   so que·m dizes, per ma fe; 20
   mais volria una calha
   estreg tener en mon se
   no faria un polhe
   qu'estes en autrui sarralha,
   c'atendes la lor merce; 25
   car soven, so cug, badalha
   qui s'aten a l'autrui be."

⁸Though one may also translate "mourning has entered into Aunis," Levy, *PD*, p. 215, lists "commencer" as a meaning of *intrar*. This sense is more satisfying here. See Textual Notes.
⁹Probably Ebles II of Ventadorn, the Singer; see Life of the Author.
¹⁰William died in Santiago de Compostela, the shrine of St. James, while on pilgrimage.

Debate Poem

2.

1. "Since every day I see love,
   Enjoyment, and amusement decline,
   And since the clergy does not help me,
   I cannot help consoling myself
   As does the swan when he knows he is dying,   5
   Who shrieks and cries
   And must send forth his song,¹
   For it is time for his life to end,
   And there is no further hope."

2. "Master, God help me,   10
   What you say is indeed appropriate;
   But do not worry about the fact
   That the clerks are of no help,
   For I believe the good season is coming
   When you will have an engagement   15
   Which will give you a saddle horse,
   Or even more valuable revenue:
   For the Count of Poitiers² is coming."

3. "Guilhalmi, by my faith, I don't care
   A cent for what you tell me;   20
   I'd rather hold a quail
   Tightly in my lap
   Than a chicken
   That might be under someone else's lock--
   That's how I'd wait for their kindness;   25
   For he who expects another's generosity
   Often waits in vain, I think."

4. "Maïstre, gran benanansa
podetz aver si sofretz."
"Guilhalmi, vostra vanansa   30
non crei, si com vos dizetz."
"Maïstre, car no·m crezetz?
Gran be vos venra de Fransa
si atendre lo voletz."
"Guilhalmi, tal esperansa   35
vos don Dieus com vos m'ufretz."

5. "Maïstre, n'ajatz coratge
d'efan ni d'ome leugier."
"Guilhalmi, sobre bon guatge
vos creyria volontier."   40
"Maïstre, man bon destrier
an li home de paratge
per sufertar al derrier."
"Guilhalmi, fort e salvatge
. . . ."   45

6. "Maïstre, josca la brosta
vos pareisa·l teit novel."
"Guilhalmi, be pauc vos costa
lo mieus ostals del castel."
"Maïstre, conte novel   50
aurem nos a Pantacosta,
que·us pagara ben e bel."
"Guilhalmi, fols qui·us escota:
vos pagatz d'autrui borcel."

Rejected readings of R: 6. crida   7. Et enuou   8. Car
li c.; vida   21. calla   30, 35. Guihelmi   31. v. me
dizetz   44. *there is a space after* fort *and after* salvate
[sic]   45. *lacking*   48. be par pauc   54. vos mi p.

4. "Master, you can have
   Great benefit if you are patient."
   "Guilhalmi, I don't believe   30
   Your vain boasting as you tell it."
   "Master, why don't you believe me?
   Great benefit will come to you from France[3]
   If you want to wait for it."
   "Guilhalmi, may God give you   35
   The kind of hope you are offering me."

5. "Master, don't have the heart
   Of a child or a frivolous man."
   "Guilhalmi, on good collateral
   I would gladly believe you."   40
   "Master, men of nobility
   Have many a good horse
   For being patient to the end."
   "Guilhalmi, strong and fierce
   . . . ."   45

6. "Master, near the foliage
   May your new roof appear."
   "Guilhalmi, my castle lodging
   Costs you very little."
   "Master, we shall have   50
   A new count[4] at Pentecost
   Who will pay you well and handsomely."
   "Guilhalmi, he is a fool who listens to you:
   You pay out of another's purse."

[1]*Per fort* is idiomatic for "of necessity" (Levy, *PD*, p. 196), and has been translated by "must".
[2]Louis VII; see 1.38, and Textual Notes.
[3]See Textual Notes.
[4]This could also be translated "account."

3. QANT LA DOUCH'AURA S'AMARCIS

1. Qant la douch'aura s'amarcis,
   e·l fuoilla chai de sul verzan,
   e l'aucel chanjan lor latis,
   ez ieu de sai sospir e chan
   d'amor qi·m ten lachat e pres,   5
   q'ieu anch no l'hagui en poder.

2. Lass! q'ieu d'amor no hai conquis
   mas can lo trebaill e l'affan;
   ni res tan grieu no·s convertis
   com fai cho q'ieu vauc desziran;   10
   ni tal enveia no·m fai res
   con fai cho q'ieu non puosc haver.

3. Per una joia m'esbaudis,
   fina, q'anch ren no amei tan;
   qant son ab lei si m'esbaïs   15
   q'eu no·ill sai dire mon talan,
   e qant m'en vauc vejaire m'es
   qe tot perda·l sen e·l saber.

4. Tota la gencer q'anc hom viz
   encontra lei no prez un gan;   20
   qan tot lo siegles brunezis,
   delai on il es si resplan;
   Dieu prejarai q'anquar la·m des,
   o qe la vei'anar jaser.

5. Totz tressaill e bram e fremis   25
   per s'amor, dormen e veillan;
   tal paor hai q'ieu mesfaillis,

Love Song

3.

1. When the sweet air grows bitter,
   And the leaf falls from the branch,
   And the birds change their chatter,
   I also sigh and sing here
   Of love which holds me tied and bound,   5
   For I have never had it in my power.

2. Alas! I have never gained anything from love
   Except the suffering and the anguish,
   And nothing is so hard to win over
   As that which I desire;[1]   10
   And nothing fills me with such desire
   As does that which I cannot have.

3. I exult for a fine jewel,
   And nothing have I ever loved as much;
   When I am with her, I am so overcome   15
   That I cannot tell her my desire;
   And when I go away, it seems to me
   That I may completely lose my sense and my mind.

4. The most beautiful woman ever seen
   Is not worth a glove compared to her;   20
   When all the world grows dark,
   It is radiant where she is;
   I will pray to God that he may still give her to me,
   Or that I may see her going to bed.

5. I shake, shiver, and tremble   25
   For her love, asleep and awake;
   I am so afraid of failing,

no m'aus pessar con la deman;
mais servir l'ai dos ansz o tres,
e puois be leu sabra·n lo ver.   30

6. No muor ne viu e no guaris,
    e mal non sen e si l'hai gran,
    qar de s'amor no soi devis;
    no sai si ja l'haurai ni qan;   35
    q'en leis es tota la merces
    qe·m pod sorzer o deschaszer.

7. Bel m'es qant il m'afolletis,
    e·m fai badar, e·n vau muszan;
    de leis m'es bel si m'escharnis,
    o·m gaba derers o denan;   40
    q'apres lo mal me venrra·l bes
    be leu, s'a leis ve a plaszer.

8. S'ella no·m vol, volgra moris
    lo dia qe·m pres en coman;
    hai lass! tan soavet m'aucis   45
    qan de s'amor mi fesz scemblan;
    qe tornat m'ha en tal deves,
    qe nuill autra no voill veszer.

9. Totz cossiros soi e jaucis,
    qar s'ieu la doptei o la blan,   50
    per lei serai o fals o fis,
    o dreichurers o ples d'enjan,
    o totz villa o totz cortes,
    o trabaillos o de leszer.

10. Mais cui qe plaja o cui qe pes,   55
    ela·m pod, si·s vol, retener.

11. Cercalmont ditz: greu er cortes
    hom qe d'amor se desesper.

1. l'aura doussa CIKR; dolzana D   2. e fuoilla L;

42

      That I don't dare think of how to ask for her;[2]
      But I will serve her for two or three years,
      And then perhaps she will know the truth.   30

6. I do not live or die or am cured,
    Or feel pain, and yet it is great,
    For I can guess nothing about her love,[3]
    I do not know when or if I shall have it;
    For in her is all the mercy   35
    That can raise me up or cast me down.

7. I love it when she drives me crazy
    And makes me gape, dreaming;[4]
    I love it when she mocks me
    Or makes fun of me openly or behind my back;   40
    For after the bad will come the good
    Soon, if I succeed in pleasing her.[5]

8. If she does not want me, I wish I had died
    The day she took me in command;
    Alas! how sweetly she killed me   45
    When she gave me her look of love;
    For she confined me in such a way
    That I wish to see no other.

9. I am very anxious, and rejoice so,
    For if I fear or flatter her,   50
    Through her shall I be false or true,
    In the right or full of deceit,
    Completely base or courtly,
    In suffering or in happiness.

10. But despite whom it may please or weigh upon,   55
     She may, if she wishes, retain me.

11. Cercamon says: it will be difficult
     For a man who despairs of love to be courtly.

[1]*Anar* followed by the present infinitive is idiomatic

desus v. DIKLa   3. l'aucels L; chanton CRa; chanta(n)
en DIK   4. desospir e dechan La   5. D'amors L   6. (Et,
Ni) ancar non l'a(i)c CDIKR   8. mas tan L; las trebalhas C
DIKR   9. non c. CDIKR   10. so qu'om plus va(i) CDIKR
10-12. *lacking in* a   11. no(n) fai CDIKR   12. aquo (aso
IK) qu'om no pot CDIKR   13. Pero (Per so IK) d'un joi m'en
esjauzis CDIKR   14. D'una q.' CDIKR   15-20. *lacking in* La
21. Quar tot CR; siegle L   22. D. om es L   23. D. mi res-
pieyt tro qu'ieu l'agues CDIKR; l'ades a   27. que no·m (non
DIK) falhis CDIKR   28. No say p. CDIKR   29. s. l'a IK
30. sabrai lo v. CDIKR   31. ne vio L   37. Gaug (n') ai
s'elha CDIKR; qant el La   38. fai muzar o(·m) vau(c) ba-
dan CDIKR   39. Et es me bel CDIKR   40. E·m torn' atras
o vauc (dereires o DIK) enan CDIKR   42. Ben tost s'a CDIKR
44. a coman CDIKR   45. Ai Dieus quan CDIKR   47. Quar
mort m'a (m'a mort DIK) e no sai per qu'es CDIKR   48. Qu'
ieu mas una no v. CDIKR; v. aver C   49-50. *lacking in* CDIKR
49. m'en esjauzis a   50. e la blan La   51. totz fals CD
IKR   52. O vertadiers o p. CDIKR   54. O trebalhiers CDI
KR; o plan deman C; plens d'affan DIK   55-56. *lacking in* D
IKR   55. Las cuy C   56. si·l vol enrequir a; enriquer L
57-58. *lacking in* La   58. qui d'amor C

4. AB LO TEMPS QE·S FAI REFRESCHAR

1. Ab lo temps qe·s fai refreschar
   lo segle e·[ls pratz] reverdezir,
   vueil un novel chant comenzar
   d'un'amor cui am e dezir;
      mas tant s'es de mi loignada   5
   q'ieu non la puesc acoseguir,
      ni de mos digz no s'agrada.

2. Ja mai res no·m pot conortar;
   abanz mi laissaratz morir,
   can m'an fag de mi donz sebrar   10
   lauzenjador, cui Deus azir!
      Las! tan l'aurai dezirada
   qe per lei plaing, plor, e sospir,
      e vau cum res enaurada.

and synonymous with the present indicative.
   ²Also possibly "ask for it," i.e. her love.
   ³For this use of *devis* see Jaufre Rudel, 6.27.
   ⁴See note 1.
   ⁵Also possibly, "soon, if it comes to please her."

Love Song

4.

1. With the season which renews
   The world, and makes the meadows green again,
   I wish to begin a new song
   About a love which I desire;
      But she is so distant from me   5
   That I cannot reach her,
      Nor does she take pleasure in my words.

2. Nothing can ever comfort me;
   Rather, let me die
   When they have separated me from my lady--   10
   Slanderers, God hate them!
      Alas! I will have desired her so much,
   That for her I lament, weep, and sigh,
   And I act as if I were out of my mind.

3. Aqesta don m'auzet[z] chantar   15
   es plus bella q'ieu no sai dir;
   fresc'a color e bel esgar,
   et es blancha ses brunezir;
     oc, e non es vernisada,
   ni om de leis non pot mal dir,   20
     tant es fina [et] esmerada.

4. E sobre tota·s deu prezar
   de dic ver, segon mon albir,
   d'ensegnamen e de parlar,
   c'anc non volc son amic traïr;   25
     et ieu fols [fui] la vegada
   car crezei ren q'en auzis dir,
     ni·l fis so don fos irada.

5. Anc ieu de lei non volc clamar,
   q'enqer, si·s vol, me pot jauzir,   30
   et a ben poder de donar
   d'aqo on me pot enrequir;
     no posc far lonja durada,
   qe·l manjar en pert e·l durmir,
     car no m'es plus aizinada.   35

6. Amors es douza al mirar
   et amara al departir;
   q'en un jorn vos fara plorar,
   et autre jogar e burdir;
     q'eu sai d'amor enseigniada: 40
   on plus la cujava servir,
     ilh es vas mi cambiada.

7. Messatges, vai, si Deus ti guar,
   e sapchas ab mi donz furmir,
   q'eu non puesc lonjamen estar   45
   [de] sai vius ni de lai guerir,
     si josta mi despoliada
   non la puesc baizar e tenir
     dinz cambra encortinada.

Rejected readings of a: 3. Veil   10. sobrar   32. enquerir

46

3. She whom you hear me sing about   15
    Is more beautiful than I can say:
    She has a fresh color and a lovely look,
    And has an unobscured radiance;
        Yes, and she is not all made up,
    And one cannot say a bad thing about her,   20
        So fine and perfect is she.

4. And she should prize herself above each,
    In my opinion, for her words
    Of truth, eloquence, and cultivation,
    For she never wished to betray her lover;   25
        And I was a fool that time
    Because I believed what I heard about her,
        And did something that angered her.

5. I have never wanted to complain about her,
    For if she wishes, she can still gladden me,   30
    And indeed she has the power to give
    Something that can enrich me;
        I cannot last very long,
    For I am not eating and am losing sleep
        Because she is not nearer to me.   35

6. Love is sweet at first sight,[1]
    And bitter at departing;
    For one day it can make you cry,
    And another it can make you play and dance;
        And I know about educated love: 40
    Just when I thought I was best serving her,
        That's when she changed toward me.

7. Messenger, go, and may God keep you;
    Get through to my lady,
    For I cannot last long   45
    Here, nor be healed from there,
        If I cannot kiss and hold her
    Naked next to me
        In a room with curtains.

---

[1]Jeanroy's translation "à l'entrée" is based on Dejeanne's emendation of *al mirar* to *a l'intrar*.

5. PER FIN'AMOR M'ESJAUZIRA

1. Per fin'amor m'esjauzira,
   tant quant fai chaut ni s'esfrezis;
   toz tems serai vas lei aclis,
   mas non puosc saber enqera
   si poirai ab joi remaner, 5
   o·m voldra per seu retener
   cella cui mos cors dezira.

2. Seignors e dompnas gerpira
   s'a lei plagues q'eu li servis;
   e qi·m diria m'en partis 10
   faria·m morir desera,
   q'en autra non ai mon esper,
   nuoit ni jorn, ni maitin ni ser,
   ni d'als mos cors non consira.

3. Ges tant leu no l'enqesira 15
   s'eu sabes cant greu s'afranquis;
   anc res no fo no s'umelis
   vas amor; mas ill n'es fera;
   e domna non pot ren valer,
   per riqessa ni per poder, 20
   se joi d'amor no l'aspira.

4. Ja de sos pes no·m partira
   s'il plagues ni m'o consentis,
   o sol que d'aitant m'enrequis
   que dixes que ma domna era, 25
   e del plus fos al seu placer,
   de la menzonja o del ver,
   c'ab sol son diz m'enrequira.

Love Song

5.

1. I would rejoice for true love
   No matter how hot or cold it was;
   I shall always submit to her,
   But I still do not know
   If I can stay in joy,   5
   Or whether she whom my heart desires
   Will wish to retain me as her own.

2. I would abandon lords and ladies
   If it pleased her that I should serve her;
   And whoever told me I should have to leave her   10
   Would cause me to die instantly,
   For I have hope in none other,
   Night or day, morning or evening,
   Nor do I[1] think of anything else.

3. I would hardly have so swiftly sought her   15
   Had I known how hard it would be to win her;
   There was never anything that did not defer
   To love; but she is haughty about it;
   And a lady cannot be worth a thing,
   Either in wealth or in power,   20
   If the joy of love does not inspire her.

4. I would never part from her feet[2]
   If it pleased her, and if she let me do so,
   Or if she enriched me only by so much
   As to tell me that she was my lady,   25
   And in addition that I was to her liking,
   (Whether she were lying or telling the truth),
   For with just her words she would make me rich.

5. Entre joi remaing et ira
   ades quant denan lei partis,   30
   q'anc pois no la vi q'ela·m dis
   qe si l'ames, mi amera;
   mas eu no sai lo seu voler;
   mas ben pot ma domna saber
   q'eu morrai si ganre·m tira.   35

6. Gencer en est mon no·s mira,
   bell'e blancha plus c'us hermis,
   plus fresca que rosa ne lis;
   ren als no m'en desespera;
   hai! si poirai l'ora veder   40
   q'eu puosca pres de llei jacer!
   eu non, qar vas mi no·s vira.

7. Toz mos talenz m'aëmplira
   ma domna, sol d'un bais m'aizis,
   q'en guerrejera mos vezis,   45
   e fora larcs, e donera,
   e·m fera grazir e temer,
   e mos enemics bas chader,
   e tengra·l meu e·l garnira.

8. E pot ben ma domna saber   50
   que ja nulz hom de mon poder
   de meillor cor no·ill servira.

9. E si·m fezes tant de placer
   qe·m laisses pres de si jaser,
   ja d'aquest mal non morira.   55

1. m'esjauzire D; m'esbaudirai f   2. ni reverdieis f
3. Et estaray tos tems aclins f   7. mon cor D   8. d. gequira f   10. q. dezia f   11. morir alera f   12. Qu'en ren als non ay mon voler f   14. Ni als mon cors non dezira; mon cor D   15. Aitant 1. f   16. cant leu D   19. Mas en donna non pot pres aver f   20. ni per aver f   24. E sivals d'aitant f   32. l' *lacking in* D   33. Alre non sai del sieu voler f   34. Mas ben pot per vertat saber f   35. s'alor s'avira f   36. Genser domna el mont no·us mira f; es mon D   37. Guai e blanca coma ermis f   40-41. Dieus si poiray l'ora vezer / qu'ieu josta leis puesca

50

5. I exist between joy and grief
   As soon as I part from her,   30
   And I have not seen her since she said to me
   That if I loved her, she would love me;
   But I do not know her desire;
   Still, my lady should know indeed
   That I shall die if she torments me long.   35

6. None nobler in this world can be seen:
   Lovely and whiter than an ermine,
   Fresher than a rose or a lily;
   Nothing else discourages me;
   Ah! if I could only see the hour   40
   When I could lie next to her!
   Not me, for she does not turn my way.

7. My lady would fulfill all my desires
   Were she to favor me with just a kiss,
   And I would wage war on my neighbors for it,   45
   And would be generous, and would give;
   I would become loved and feared,
   And would lay my enemies low,
   And would hold my possessions and enrich them.[3]

8. And my lady may know for certain   50
   That never would a man of my power
   Serve her with a better heart.

9. And if she caused me so much pleasure
   As to let me lie next to her,
   Never would I die from this pain.   55

    [1]*Mos cors* can be idiomatic for "I" or "myself," and need not be translated here.
    [2]Also possibly "I would never part from her thoughts."
    [3]*Fera* and *tengra* might also have "she" as subject.

jazer f   42. Ben ai dreg mas trop mi tira f   43. m'
lacking in f   47. E fera·m blandir f   49. E·m tengra
miels e·n guarnira f   50-55. *lacking in* f

6. ASSATZ ES ORA OIMAI Q'EU CHANT

1. Assatz es ora oimai q'eu chant;
    tant ai estat acondurmitz
    c'anc mos chanz non fon lueing auzitz;
    mas era·m vau ja reveilhant,
    et irei mon joi recobran   5
    contre l'ivern e·l freig aurei.

2. De joi no·m cal [fugir] enan,
    c'anc un sol jorn no·n fui garnitz;
    et es m'al cor prion sorzitz,
    si q'entre gens vau sospiran   10
    lo dezirier c'ai d'amor gran;
    ni dorm ni veil, ni aug ni vei.

3. S'anc per amor anei veilhan,
    ni·n fui anc fols ni trassailitz,
    ni cambïatz per chamjaritz,   15
    era·n lau Dieu e Saint Joan,
    c'ab tal amor vau amoran
    c'anc non chamjec per autre mei.

4. Cesta non cug qe ja m'[engan],
    s'ieu ja de leis no soi garnitz;   20
    ni no·n soi tant afolatitz
    qe ja re·il qeira ni·l deman,
    petit ni pro, ni tan ni qant,
    ni mal ni be, ni re ni qei.

5. Tant la sei coinda e prezan,   25
    e·l faigz de leis es tant eslitz,
    qe sai me tenc per enreqitz,

Love Song

6.

1. The time has come for me to sing;
   I have been so asleep
   That my song has not been heard afar;
   But now I am awake,
   And I shall regain my joy   5
   In spite of the winter and the cold wind.

2. I should not run away from joy,
   For I have never for a day been graced with it;
   And it has surged deeply in my heart,
   So that among people I sigh   10
   For the great desire of love that I have;
   I neither sleep nor wake, hear nor see.

3. If ever I stayed awake for love,
   Or was a fool or betrayed because of it,
   Or was crossed by a fickle woman,   15
   Now I praise God and Saint John
   Because I love with such a love
   That never exchanged me for another.[1]

4. I do not believe that this one would cheat me,
   Though I have not yet been graced by her;   20
   Nor am I so foolish
   As ever to seek or ask anything of her,
   Small or large, this or that,
   Bad or good, or anything.

5. I know her to be so gracious and dignified,   25
   And her deeds are of such high merit,
   That here I consider myself rich,

       e lai [serai en] son coman
       la nueg e·l jorn e·l mes e l'an,
       c'aissi soi sieus con esser dei.   30

6.   Plas es lo vers, vauc l'afinan
     ses mot vila, fals, apostitz;
     et es totz enaissi noiritz
     c'ap motz politz lo vau uzan;
     e tot ades va·s meilluran   35
     s'es qi be·l chant ni be·l desplei.

Rejected readings of a: 5. recobram   9. so ditz
10. sens vau   18. no·m ch.   27. enqeritz   28. E lai
a hiu la coman   35. meilluram

             7. AB LO PASCOR M'ES BEL Q'EU CHANT

1.   Ab lo pascor   m'es bel q'eu chant
     en estiu, a l'entran de mai,
     can par la flor   sobre·l verchant,
     e son reverdezit li glai:
     mout mi val pauc lo temps cortes,   5
     q'eu non ai joi, ni non l'ades,
     ni de sa compagnia no·m lau.

2.   Per qe d'amor   an atretan--
     li malvas, enojos savai--
     con li meillor   e·l plus prezan;   10
     Jovenz, e Faig, fraing e dechai,
     e Malvestatz a son luec pres
     en amistatz, c'amics non es
     amatz, ni d'amigua no·s jau.

3.   Ben sai qe lor   es mal estan   15
     als molleiratz, car se fan gai
     domnejador   ni drudejan;
     e·l guizardos qe lor n'eschai

                            54

And there [I shall be in] her command
Any night, day, month, or year,
For I am hers as I ought to be.   30

6. The song is plain, and I perfect it
   Without a vile, false, bastardized word;
   And it has been worked over to the point
   That I practise it with polished words;
   And it still continues to improve   35
   If there's one to sing or perform it well.

[1]This line may also mean "that never changed me for other than I am." Compare this stanza with Jaufre Rudel, Poem 5, especially lines 31-32.

Satiric Love Song[1]

7.

1. At Eastertime I love to sing
   In summer, at the beginning of May,
   When the flower appears on the branch,
   And the sword-lilies are again in bloom;
   (But) the courtly season is worth little to me,   5
   For I neither have, nor get close to joy,
   And I don't boast of its company.

2. For they have just as much of love--
   The base, aggravating good-for-nothings--
   As do the best and most worthy;   10
   Youth and Deeds break down and decline,
   And Baseness has taken its place
   In love affairs, for a lover is not
   Loved, nor enjoys a beloved.

3. I know well that it is indecent   15
   That husbands become wild
   Womanizers and courters;
   And the reward that they get for it

        ditz el reprocher lo pajes:
        qi glazi fai, a glazi es   20
        feritz d'eis lo seu colp mortau.

4.   Fals amador, al meu semblan,
        vostr'er lo danz, e no·n pueis mai;
        de gran folor   es acordan
        can l'us l'autre gali'e trai;   25
        e pos vos [o] aves enqes,
        drut, moiller e marit--tug tres--
        sias del pechat comunau.

5.   El fuec major   seretz creman,
        al juzizi del derrer plai,   30
        enganador   fel deslian,
        en la pena qe non trasvai,
        on sera totz lo mals e·l bes
        jutjatz, e [ja] no·m clam merces
        domna c'aia drut desleiau.   35

6.   Non a valor   d'aissi enan
        cela c'ab dos ni ab tres jai,
        et ai! n'encor   lo cor tristan
        qe Dieus tan falsa non fetz sai;
        miels li fora ja non nasqes,   40
        enanz qe failliment f[ez]es
        don er parlat tro en Peitau.

7.   Saint Salvador, fai m'albergan
        lai el regne on mi donz estai,
        ab la genzor, si q'en baizan   45
        sien nostre coven verai;
        e qe·m do zo qe m'a promes;
        pueis al jorn m'en ira[i] conqes,
        si be l'es mal al gelos brau.

8.   Amics, diguas li·m can la ves,   50
        si passa·l terme q'avem pres,
        q'ieu soi mo[r]tz, per Sain Nicolau!

56

           The countryman tells of in his proverb:
           Whoever takes the sword, with the sword   20
           Is struck by his own mortal blow.

    4.   False lovers, in my opinion,
           Yours will be the loss, and I cannot help it;
           It is to consent to great folly
           When one cheats and betrays another;   25
           And since you have asked for it,
           Lover, wife, and husband--all three--
           May you be joined together in sin.

    5.   In the great fire you shall burn,
           At the judgment of the Last Court,   30
           Recreant, disrupting deceivers,
           In the pain which does not abate,
           Where all the bad and good
           Shall be judged, and let a lady who has
           An unfaithful lover not cry to me for mercy.   35

    6.   Worthless from now on is she
           Who sleeps with two or three,
           And ah! I gain a heavy heart because of it,[2]
           For God never created a falser one here;
           It would have been better if she had not been born, 40
           Rather than that she commit a sin
           That will be gossiped of as far as Poitou.

    7.   Holy Savior, give me lodging
           There in the land where my lady stays,
           With the noblest one, so that in kissing,   45
           Our agreements may be fulfilled;
           And let her give me what she promised;
           Then at daybreak I shall go away won over,[3]
           Though it sits ill with the rude, jealous man.

    8.   Friend, tell her for me when you see her,   50
           If the time we agreed on passes by,
           That I am dead, by St. Nicholas!

57

Rejected readings of a: 3. flors sobre·ls   7. non lau
27. moillerat   29. arden   31. desliau   35. donna
38. ai n'enqer   43. Salvaire   45. genzer   48. j.
s'en   50. dignas

8. PUS NOSTRE TEMPS COMENS'A BRUNEZIR

1. Pus nostre temps comens'a brunezir,
   e li verjan son de lor fuelhas blos,
   e del solelh vey tant bayssatz los rays,
   per que·l jorn son escur e tenebros,
   et hom non au d'auzelhs ni chans ni lays,   5
   per joy d'amor nos devem esbaudir.

2. Aquest'amor no pot hom tan servir
   que mil aitans no·n doble·l gazardos;
   que pretz e joys e tot quant es, e mays,
   n'auran aisselh qu'en seran poderos;   10
   qu'anc non passet covinens ni los frays--
   mas per semblan greus er a conquerir.

3. Per lieys deu hom esperar e sofrir,
   tant es sos pretz valens e cabalos;
   qu'anc non ac suenh dels amadors savays,   15
   de ric escas ni de paubr'ergulhos;
   qu'en plus de mil non a dos tan verays
   que fin'amors los deya obezir.

4. Ist trobador, entre ver e mentir,
   afollon drutz e molhers et espos,   20
   e van dizen qu'amors vay en biays,
   per que·l marit en devenon gilos,
   e donas son intradas em pantays;
   cuy mout vol hom escoutar et auzir.

5. Sist sirven fals fan a plusors gequir   25

¹Rita Lejeune believes that this poem was composed in the Holy Land ca. 1147, and refers to the scandal of Eleanor of Aquitaine; see Life of the Author.
²Lejeune followed Appel and Kolsen in seeing the medieval hero in *tristan*. For this whole line see Textual Notes.
³See Textual Notes.

Satiric Love Song

8.

1. Since our season begins to grow dark,
   And the branches are bare of their leaves,
   And I see the sun's rays so low
   That the days are dark and shadowy,
   And from the birds one hears no songs or lays,   5
   For joy of love we should be glad.

2. One cannot serve this love so much
   That its reward will not redouble a thousand times;
   For distinction and joy and everything, and more,
   Those who are capable of it shall have;   10
   For it never went back on promises or broke them--
   But it seems it will be difficult to conquer.

3. For it one should hope and suffer,
   So excellent and superior is its distinction;
   And it has never cared for worthless lovers,   15
   For a stingy noble or a wretched proud man;
   And in a thousand there are hardly two so true
   That true love should obey them.

4. These troubadours, between truth and falsehood,
   Confound lovers and wives and husbands,   20
   And say that love is devious,
   So that husbands become jealous because of it,
   And ladies have begun to get ideas;
   (And) one gladly listens to and hears them.

5. These false servants cause many to abandon   25

Pretz, e Joven elonhar ad estros,
don Proeza no cug que sia mais,
qu'Escassedatz ten las claus dels baros;
manhs n'a serratz din la ciutat d'Abays,
don Malvestatz no·n layssa un yssir.   30

6. Ves manhtas partz vey lo segle fallir,
   per qu'ieu n'estauc marritz e cossiros
   que soudadiers non truep ab cuy s'apays,
   per lauzengiers qu'an bec malahuros,
   qui son pejor que Judas, que Dieus trays: 35
   ardre·ls degr'om e totz vius sebellir!

7. Nos no·ls podem castiar ni cobrir;
   tollam nos d'elhs, e Dieus accoselh nos,
   q'us joys d'amor me reverdis e·m pays,
   e puesc jurar qu'anc ta bella no fos;   40
   petit la vey, mas per ella suy gays,
   e jauzions, e Dieus m'en do jauzir.

8. Ara·s pot hom lavar et esclarzir
   de gran blasme, silh que son encombros;
   e si es pros, yssira ves Roays,   45
   e gurpira lo segle perilhos;
   et ab aitan pot si liurar del fays
   qu'assatz en fai trabucar e perir.

9. Fagz es lo vers, e non deu veillezir,
   segon aisso qe monstra la razos,   50
   q'anc bon'amors non galiet ni trais;
   anz dona joi als arditz amoros.

10. Cercamonz diz: qi vas amors s'irais,
    meravill'es com pot l'ira suffrir;
    q'ira d'amor es paors et esglais,   55
    e no·n pot hom trop viure ni murir.

2. las f. CR; la foilla a   3. baissar a   5. voutas
ni 1. A   6. nos deu om a   11. ni·ls estrais A; e(s)-
frais DIKa   12. greus es a   14. Tant er A   16. de

60

      Distinction, and to alienate Youth completely,
      And so I think that Excellence can no longer exist,
      For Stinginess holds the barons' keys;
      Many has he locked in the City of Decadence,
      (And) from there Baseness lets not one escape.   30

6.   Everywhere I see the world decline,
      And so I am saddened and concerned
      That the mercenary finds no one to feed him,
      Thanks to slanderers who have a wicked tongue,
      Who are worse than Judas, who betrayed God: 35
      One should burn them and bury them alive!

7.   We cannot either correct or excuse them;
      Let us get away from them, and God help us,
      For a joy from love refreshes and feeds me,
      And I can swear there was never one so lovely;   40
      I see her little, but for her I am merry,
      And joyful, and may God give me her to enjoy.

8.   Now one can cleanse and purify oneself[1]
      Of great blame--those who are encumbered--
      And if one is worthy he will leave for Edessa,[2]   45
      And will abandon the perilous world;
      And thus he can throw off the burden[3]
      Which makes many fall down and perish.

9.   The song is done, and it should not age,
      According to what the matter shows,   50
      For good love never cheated or betrayed,
      Rather it gives joy to steadfast lovers.

10. Cercamon says: whoever becomes angry with love,
      It is amazing how he can suffer the torment;
      For the torment of love is fear and terror,   55
      And in it one cannot really either live or die.

---

[1] Cf. Marcabru's *vers del lavador*, *Pax in nomine Domini!*
[2] Edessa fell to the Moslems in 1144; see Life of the Author.
[3] See Jaufre Rudel, 2.56, and Marcabru, *Ans que·l terminis*, 21: *Ben es cargatz de fol fais / qui d'amor es en pantais.*

ric estar a   17. non a uns a   18. lo deya Ca
19. Li trobador C   21. c'a. nais A; c'a. torn'em a
24. car trop volon e. a   26. J. e donar a   29. de(1)
bais ACDIK   31-56. *lacking in* ADIK   31-48. *lacking in* a
49-56. *lacking in* C   49. Fagz el a   51. g. ni frais a
53. qe vas a

Textual Notes

MANUSCRIPTS

A - Rome, Bibl. Vaticana, lat. 5232 (13th c. Italy)
C - Paris, Bibl. Nationale, fr. 856 (14th c., S. France)
D - Modena, Bibl. Estense, R.4.4, Estero 45 (13th and 14th
    cc., Italy)
I - Paris, Bibl. Nationale, fr. 854 (13th c., Italy)
K - Paris, Bibl. Nationale, fr. 12473 (13th c., Italy)
L - Rome, Bibl. Vaticana, lat. 3206 (14th c., Italy)
R - Paris, Bibl. Nationale, fr. 22543 (14th c., S. France)
a - Modena, Bibl. Estense, Campori, App. 426, 427, 494, N.8.4
    11-13 (16th c. Italian copy of a (probably) early 14th c.
    MS written by the S. French scribe Bernart Amoros)
f - Paris, Bibl. Nationale, fr. 12474 (14th c., S. France)

1. LO PLAING COMENZ IRADAMEN

(Pillet-Carstens 112.2a)

Manuscript: a, pp. 369-70 (transcribed in Bertoni (1901), 425).
Attributions to others: None.
Major editions: Dejeanne, No. 7, p. 55; Jeanroy, No. 6, p. 19.
Structure: 9 6-line stanzas, each with different rhymes, except last line the same in all (*coblas singulars*).
Meter and rhyme: 8 aaaaax, bbbbbx, etc.
This song was most likely written in the spring of 1137, shortly after the death of William X of Aquitaine, on April 9.

5. *Malvestatz:* "Evil" and "Wickedness" are too strong to convey the sense of this word. First used by Cercamon and Marcabru, it denotes the good-for-nothing, cowardly, bad nature of powerful barons, who are morally degenerate, and can hardly be interesting enough to be really evil.

9. *li Barrau:* Jeanroy suggests that the *Barrau* are the people of Bar-sur-Seine, and by extension the Burgundians. By the marriage of William VIII, grandfather of William X, to a daughter of Robert of Burgundy, the dukes of Aquitaine possessed several fiefs in Burgundy. These fiefs went to William X's second daughter, Petronilla (see quote from William's will, note to line 38). Cercamon's mention of Poitou in line 8 may be meant to go with his mention of the *Barrau*, or Burgundians, in line 9, since just as Petronilla had been given the Burgundian fiefs, so Eleanor had been given Poitou, as well as the rest of Aquitaine. So these allusions may be meant to suggest the inheritance of the two daughters. Jeanroy refers to two mentions of the *Barrau*, both times associated with *Frances* (on whom see note to line 37) in the *Chanson de la Croisade Albigeoise* (1415, 3926, ed. Meyer); see also the edition of Martin-Chabot, I, 152. Thus, it should be remembered that Cercamon's allusion is formulaic, and may not be meant as a precise historical statement.

10. [*peza·m*] was suggested by Dejeanne on the basis of line 16; *longa*[*s*] is Jeanroy's emendation; *a longas* is formulaic and invariable.

11. Jeanroy dropped the *s* of *Segners*, but the nominative form is not consistently used in the vocative case in Old

Prov.; cf. 7.43.

12. *metet[z]:* The form *-et* of the 2nd person plural is found in some MSS, and dates back to the 12th century; see Anglade, *Grammaire,* p. 270.

13. *Pitieu:* Jeanroy prints *Peitieu;* also, the MS reads *plaing,* although an inkblot has obscured the *i, pace* Jeanroy's variant.

15. *soffraing:* A complex subject governing a singular verb is not uncommon in Old Prov.; cf. 7.11, and Jaufre Rudel, 1.17-18: *Luenh es lo castelhs e la tors.* The dual subjects are formulaic.

22. Jeanroy suggests correcting *defendetz* to *defendretz* or *defendatz,* but there is no reason to suspect that *defendetz* is not properly imperative, although Jeanroy translates it as a future.

26. *paubre:* Jeanroy's emendation of *paubres;* the scribe most likely thought that *paubres* was the subject of *aten.*

29. *ver afic:* Cf. Marcabru, *Lo vers comenssa,* 16, and Guilhem de Saint-Leidier, *Estat aurai,* 48, for the meaning "Last Judgment"; see De Lollis in *Studj, 9,* 154. The phrase is found neither in Raynouard, III, 321, or Levy, *SW,* I, 26.

32. *aves:* Jeanroy prints *avez.*

35. *un non troba:* Jeanroy's emendation of *us non troba;* the scribe most likely thought that *us* was the subject of *troba;* as for *s'aiziu,* Levy, *PD,* p. 13, lists the meanings of *aizivar* as "to welcome, accomodate," and of *s'aizivar* as "to approach"; Jeanroy translates here "s'abrite"; for the forms *aizi, (s')aizinar, aizir, aizina* in William IX and in Jaufre Rudel, see Sources and Influences.

37. *Norman e Frances:* That Cercamon's mention of the Normans does not reflect recent history is suggested by the fact that the last major campaign in which William X took part was Geoffrey of Anjou's invasion of Normandy in September of 1136. For an account of the invasion from a Norman point of view see Orderic Vitalis, *Hist. Eccl.,* 13.26, ed. Chibnall, VI, 466-74. It is true that Orderic credits the invasion to the Angevins and not to the Poitevins. Orderic further recounts, 13.30, that it was to alleviate the remorse which he felt for the barbarous acts committed during the Norman expedition that William decided to go on pilgrimage to St. James. See also A. Richard, *Histoire des comtes de Poitou,* II, 50-51. It should also be noted that the Normans had supported, as had William, the cause of Anacletus in the papal schism of 1130. As for *Frances,* these are the inhabitants of the royal domain strictly speaking; cf. 2.33 and note. Jeanroy prints *Franceis* to conform visually with the

rhyme words, but this need not affect pronunciation.

38. De Lollis corrected *dieu* to *deu*. In reference to *lo reis*, in his will William X entrusted the marrying of his daughter and heiress Eleanor to Louis VI, who named his son, who became Louis VII in the same year, as her husband. Louis VII, upon the death of his father, became Duke of Aquitaine. He abandoned this title when he divorced Eleanor in 1152. William's will is copied in Bouquet, *Histoire des Gaules*, XII, 409: *Filias meas Regis domini mei protectioni relinquo, Leonoram collocandam cum domino Ludovico Regis filio, si baronibus meis placuerit, cui Aquitaniam et Pictaviam relinquo, Petronellae vero filiae meae, possessiones meas et castella quae in Burgundia, ut proles Gerardi ducis Burgundiae, possideo...*

39. Jeanroy added [*el*] before *laisset*, which retains the quasi-iambic rhythm of the line, and fills out the meter, *terra* eliding with *e·l*; *·l creis* here refers to Eleanor of Aquitaine; see previous note.

40. Jeanroy emended *tan* to *aitan* for the meter; *honor* means "lands, territory, fief," and refers to the immense fief of Aquitaine which William X had left to his suzerain Louis VI.

41. *mal estara*: Jeanroy emends this to *mal l'estara*.

42. Jeanroy emends *chivauge* (he prints *chivauje*) to *chivauchan*.

43. Jeanroy emends *pez* to *pes*.

44. *Limozi*: Since William had no male heir by his wife, Aenor of Châtellerault, on her death in 1136 he became engaged to Emma, daughter of Aymar of Limoges. This potential union alarmed the Limousins, who felt that the Count would be too powerful for comfort under such circumstances. They thus counseled William VI Taillefer of Angoulême to take her away and marry her, which he did. They might have suffered the consequences of this insult if William of Poitou had not died on pilgrimage.

48. *Aunis*: See Richard, *Histoire*, II, 15-17, for an account of how William gained control of the fief of Aunis from Isembert of Châtelaillon. Jeanroy emends *dos* to *dols*.

49. Jeanroy does not print *raggo* as a's reading.

52. De Lollis emends *de pain* to *d'Espain'*; Jeanroy adds [*cil*] for the meter.

2. CAR VEI FENIR A TOT DIA

(Pillet-Carstens 112.1)

Manuscript: R, fol. 48r.
Attributions to others: None.
Major editions: Mahn, No. 4, p. 97; Dejeanne, No. 8, p. 59; Jeanroy, No. 7, p. 23.
Structure: 6 9-line stanzas, each with different rhymes, (*coblas singulars*), except stanzas 2 and 3 which have the same rhymes (*coblas doblas*).
Meter and rhyme: 8a' 7b 8a' 7bb 8a' 7b 8a' 7b (*escota* in line 53 is an assonance).

2. [*l'amor*] is Mahn's conjecture.
6. Jeanroy corrects *crida* to *cria*.
7. Mahn corrects to *e·n mou*.
8. Jeanroy emends *car li* to *que·l* for the meter.
18. Louis came south in May, 1137, to marry Eleanor of Aquitaine; hence also the mention of *Pantacosta* in line 51. The ceremony took place on July 27 (or possibly August 1) at the cathedral of St. André in Bordeaux.
21. Jeanroy emends *calla* to *calha*; the scribe merely left out the hook of the *h*.
23. *polhe:* Cf. Marcabru, *Dirai vos en mon lati*, 25 (*poilli*).
29. Jeanroy lists *sofrez* as the reading, but the MS reads *sofretz*.
30, 35. The MS reads *Guilhelmi*; the change seems merely scribal, and we have followed Jeanroy in printing the single spelling.
31. Jeanroy emends *me dizetz* to *dizetz* for the meter.
33. *Fransa* here denotes a more restricted area than "France" today; *Fransa* referred to the royal domain, and did not include the surrounding counties; see 1.37.
46-47. Several solutions to these lines have been offered. Chabaneau proposes *fosca...no·s...*, "the husk does not seem black to the new shell," i.e. the nut is not ripe when the shell begins to form, possibly a proverbial way of saying "wait a little"; Tobler gives *josta...pareisso·1 jet*: "next to the foliage appear young offspring," i.e. the Count of Poitiers who is coming; Dejeanne has *josta...pareisso·1 teit*: "next to the foliage appear the new roofs"; Jeanroy leaves the MS as is, and does not translate. We assume that *pareisa* is a possible form of the present subjunctive of *pareiser* (cf. *teisser*, pres. subj. *teissa*). Here we have Guilhalmi's easy optimism on the subject of new lodging for himself and his "master."

48. We follow Jeanroy's emendation of *be par pauc*.
54. Jeanroy does not list *mi pagatz* in his rejected readings.

3. QANT LA DOUCH'AURA S'AMARCIS

(Pillet-Carstens 112.4)

Manuscripts: C, fol. 254r-v; D, fol. 196r-v; I, fol. 133v; K, fol. 119; L, fol. 115v-116r; R, fol. 21v; a, pp. 364-65. *Base*: L (1-14, 21-56; transcribed in Pelaez (1921), 144), D (15-20, 57-58).
Attributions to others: C (Peire Bremon Ricas Novas, but under Cercamon in the table), L (anon.).
Major editions: Mahn, No. 1, p. 91; Dejeanne, No. 2, p. 38; Jeanroy, No. 1, p. 1.
Structure: 9 6-line stanzas plus 2 tornadas, all with the same rhymes (*coblas unissonans*); stanzas 5 and 6 are reversed in CDIKR, as are stanzas 7 and 8; in C the order of tornadas is reversed.
Meter and rhyme: 8 ababcd + 8 cd + 8 cd.
For the most part, Jeanroy has used the spelling of C, but has taken the majority of substantial readings from La, as well as La's stanza order (L's text is better and more complete than a's); thus, only his substantive, not his spelling deviations from L will be recorded in detail.

1. Jeanroy prints CIKR's *Quant l'aura doussa*.
5. *d'amor* is Jeanroy's correction; for *d'amor* the scribe has followed the case system consistently in lines 7, 26, 34, 46, and 58.
21. *siegles*: Following Jeanroy and all other MSS, we have emended L's *siegle*.
23. *q'anquar la·m des*: Jeanroy prints a's *qu'ancar l'ades*.
26. *dormen e veillan*: Jeanroy prints *durmen o velhan*.
32. *mal non sen*: Jeanroy prints *mal no·m sent*.
41. *me venrra·l bes*: Jeanroy prints *me venra bes*.
44. *en coman*: Jeanroy prints CDIKR's *a coman*.
49. *soi e jaucis*: Jeanroy prints a's *m'en esjauzis*.
50. Jeanroy emends La's *e la blan* to *o la blan*, since *doptei* and *blan* are alternatives and require the disjunctive "or."

55-58. We follow Jeanroy in reversing C's order of tornadas here, because stanza 11 comes as a non-sequitur after stanza 9, whereas stanza 10 follows stanza 9 naturally, and because the tornadas of Song 8 (which we have reversed for different reasons) suggest that the formula *Cercalmont ditz* should appear in the lines which end the poem.

55. *qe plaja:* Jeanroy prints a's *que plass'*.
56. *retener:* Jeanroy adopts CDIKR's reading in place of L's weak *enriquer*, the usual form of which is *enrequir*, as in a, which violates the rhyme.
58. Jeanroy lists C's reading as *que d'amor*, but this MS reads *qui d'amor*, which Jeanroy prints.

4. AB LO TEMPS QE·S FAI REFRESCHAR

(Pillet-Carstens 112.1b)

Manuscript: a, pp. 366-67 (transcribed in Bertoni (1901), 423).
Attributions to others: None.
Major editions: Dejeanne, No. 4, p. 45; Jeanroy, No. 2, p. 4.
Structure: 7 7-line stanzas, all with the same rhymes (*coblas unissonans*).
Meter and rhyme: 8 ababc'bc'.
2. [·ls pratz] is Jeanroy's conjecture.
6. *acoseguir:* Jeanroy prints *aconseguir*.
9. *laissaratz:* De Lollis suggested *laissarai*.
10. Jeanroy emends *can* to *car*.
15. *auzet[z]:* For the form *auzet* see 1.12.
22. In the MS this line is written as part of the previous stanza.
23. *dic:* Jeanroy prints *dig*.
26. Bertoni supplied [*fui*].
27. *car crezei:* Jeanroy emends this to *can crezei*.
29. *non volc clamar:* Dejeanne emends this to *no·m volc clamar*.
32. *enrequir* is Dejeanne's emendation of the unlikely *enquerir*.
36. *al mirar:* Dejeanne emends this to *a l'intrar*.
42. *ilh es:* Jeanroy emends this to *ilh s'es*.
46. [*de*] is supplied by Dejeanne.

5. PER FIN'AMOR M'ESJAUZIRA

(Pillet-Carstens 112.3)

Manuscripts: D, fols. 196v-197r; f, fols. 43v-44r (new numbering). *Base:* D (transcribed in Mussafia (1867), 445).

Attributions to others: f (anon.).

Major editons: Dejeanne, No. 1, p. 34; Jeanroy, No. 8, p. 26.

Structure: 7 7-line stanzas plus 2 tornadas, all with the same rhymes (*coblas unissonans*); the order of stanzas in f is 1573 2(8-9)-4(24-28) 4(22-23)-2(10-14) 6.

Meter and rhyme: 8 a'bbc'dda' + 8 dda' + 8 dda'.

7, 14. *mos cors:* We have followed Jeanroy in emending *mon cor* to *mos cors*; the scribe probably took *mon cor* as object of *dezira* and *consira*.

8. Here and throughout the poem, though not with complete consistency, Jeanroy adds u after c and g (*guerpira*).

16. *greu* is Jeanroy's correction; the lady is difficult, not easy, to win.

21. Jeanroy emends *joi* to *jois*, which is not necessary.

24. *o sol que d'aitant:* Jeanroy prints f's reading *e sivals d'aitant*.

25. *dixes:* Jeanroy prints *disses*.

28. *diz:* Jeanroy prints *dig*.

30. *quant denan lei partis:* Jeanroy prints f's reading *quant de lei* (*leis* f) *mi partis*.

32. *mi amera:* Jeanroy prints f's reading *ill m'amera*.

33. *mas eu no sai lo seu voler:* Jeanroy prints f's reading *al re no* (*non* f) *sai de son* (*del sieu* f) *voler*.

36. *Gencer en est mon:* Jeanroy prints f's reading *Genser domna el mon* (*mont* f).

40. Jeanroy prints f's reading *Dieus si poirai* (*poiray* f) *l'ora veder* (*vezer* f).

6. ASSATZ ES ORA OIMAI Q'EU CHANT

(Pillet-Carstens 112.1c)

Manuscript: a, pp. 365-66 (transcribed in Bertoni (1901), 423).

Attributions to others: None.

Major editions: Dejeanne, No. 3, p. 43; Jeanroy, No. 3, p.8.

Structure: 6 6-line stanzas, all with the same rhymes (*coblas unissonans*).

Meter and rhyme: 8 abbaac.

1, 4. *chant, reveilhant:* Jeanroy prints *chan* and *reveilhan*.

5. Jeanroy emends *irei* to *irai*.

7. [*fugir*] is Jeanroy's conjecture. Bertoni suggested *deserenan*.

9. Jeanroy emends *so ditz* to *sorzitz*.
10. Jeanroy emends *entre sens* to *entre gens*.
19. [*engan*] is De Lollis' conjecture.
20. *garnitz:* Dejeanne suggested emending this to *grazitz*, probably because *garnitz* occurs in line 8; but this change is unnecessary.
24. *ni re ni qei:* Jeanroy emends this to *ni so ni qei*.
25. *Tant la sei:* Jeanroy emends this to *Tant la vei*, but this produces a weaker sense than does a's reading.
27. *enrequitz* is De Lollis' emendation of *enqueritz;* cf. 4.32.
28. [*serai en*] *son coman* is Jeanroy's conjecture and correction of *la coman*. We have not encountered another example of *coman* being feminine, as a has it; we thus treat *la* as a copyist's error.
33. *noiritz:* Jeanroy emends this to *bastitz*.
34. *uzan:* Levy, *PD*, p. 376, lists "fréquenter" as a meaning of *uzar*, and we extend the sense of "fréquenter" to include "practise," which is relevant to this context.

7. AB LO PASCOR M'ES BEL Q'EU CHANT

(Pillet-Carstens 112.1a)

Manuscript: a, pp. 367-68 (transcribed in Bertoni (1901), 424).
Attributions to others: None.
Major editions: Dejeanne, No. 5, p. 48; Jeanroy, No. 4, p. 11; Lejeune, *Romania, 83,* 186.
Structure: 7 7-line stanzas (not counting rhymed halflines), all with the same rhymes (*coblas unissonans*).
Meter and rhyme: alternative schemes: (1) 4ab 8c 4ab 8c 8dde; (2) 8 ababccd.
1, 3. *chant, verchant:* Jeanroy prints *chan, verchan*.
3. *flor:* Jeanroy prints *flors,* but *flor* here is necessary for the internal rhyme of each first and third line, first noticed by Pillet. In a this rhyme is violated at 3. *flors,* 38. *enqer,* 43. *salvaire,* and 45. *genzer;* see notes to these lines. In his preface to the songbook which is represented by a, Bernart Amoros says that he emended his exemplar in order to conform to correct language; see MS. Florence, Riccardiana 2814, p. 2. *flors, salvaire,* and *genzer* are probably his doing, and show an overriding concern for grammar in the face of prosodic constraints. For another example of *flor* nominative singular, cf. Marcabru, *Bel m'es quan son li fruich,* 37.

6. Dejeanne suggested correcting *joi* to *lei*.
7. *no·m lau* is De Lollis' emendation of *non lau*.
11. For the dual subjects *Jovenz* and *Faig* see 1.15.
12. Jeanroy lists *luecs* as a's reading, but the MS reads *luec*.
13. Jeanroy lists *amiztatz* as a's reading, but the MS reads *amistatz*; he emends to *amistat* in his text.
17. *drudejan* is probably either a verbal noun or a third person plural from the otherwise unattested **drudejar*; see Adams, *Word Formation in Provençal*, pp. 357-60.
18. *guizardos:* Jeanroy emends this to *guizardo*, taking it strictly as the object of *ditz* in the next line.
19. *reprocher:* Jeanroy emends this to *reprovier*.
20. *qi glazi fai:* De Lollis emends this to *q'a glazi fer*.
27. *moiller e marit* is Dejeanne's correction; the MS reading is shown to be incorrect by *tug tres*: *moillerat* and *marit* both denote the husband.
29. *creman* is Dejeanne's emendation, for the rhyme; cf. Marcabru, *Hueymais dey esser alegrans*, 31: *estas putas ardens, cremans*.
30, 32. Jeanroy reverses the order of these lines.
31. Dejeanne suggested emending *desliau* to *e truan*, but failed to see that the *n* of *deslian* had probably been mistaken for *u*.
34. [*ja*] is Jeanroy's conjecture; he also emends *no·m clam* to *no clam*.
38. *n'encor lo cor tristan:* The cruces *encor* and *tristan* have raised much debate. A reading in *-or*, with close *o*, is needed for the internal rhyme; Pillet's correction *encor* (*encorre*, "to incur, contract") has been adopted here. It seems unlikely, despite the view of Appel, Kolsen and Lejeune, that *tristan* refers to the medieval hero, simply because it would not make sense in this context: there is no reason why the fact that the lady is false should cause the poet to have "the heart of Tristan": Tristan was certainly never wounded by Iseult's falseness. Jeanroy prints *n'enger* and *tristan*.
41. *f[ez]es* is Pillet's correction.
43. *Salvador* is Pillet's correction; the subject case for the vocative is not consistently used in Old Prov., and *Salvador* is necessary here for the internal rhyme. Jeanroy prints *Salvaire*.
45. *genzor* is De Lollis' correction; both grammar and rhyme require *genzor*, which Jeanroy prints.
48. *m'en ira[i]:* The MS reading *s'en ira conges*, which Jeanroy prints, cannot stand, as *s'* refers back to a feminine antecedent, requiring *conqiza*. Dejeanne suggested *con q'es*

"as she is," but the result was obscure. Because of the traditional *alba* situation here, *m'en ira[i]* is offered to preserve grammar and logical consistency.

8. PUS NOSTRE TEMPS COMENS'A BRUNEZIR

(Pillet-Carstens 112.3a)

Manuscripts: A, fol. 142v; C, fols. 359v-360r; D, fol. 186r; I, fol. 111r; K, fol. 96r; a, pp. 368-69. *Base:* C (1-48), a (49-56, with order of tornadas reversed; transcribed in Bertoni (1904), 78).
Attributions to others: ADIK (Peire Bremon Ricas Novas).
Major editions: Mahn, No. 3, p. 96; Dejeanne, No. 6, p. 52; Jeanroy, No. 5, p. 14.
Structure: 8 6-line stanzas plus 2 tornadas, all with the same rhymes (*coblas unissonans*).
Meter and rhyme: 10 abcbca + 10 abcb + 10 caca.
The mention of the departure for Edessa suggests that this song was written ca. 1147. See Life of the Author.
    1. *Pus:* Jeanroy prints *Puois*.
    2. *lor fuelhas:* We follow Jeanroy in rejecting C's *las fuelhas* as a *lectio facilior*, in favor of the reading of ADIK.
    11. *ni los frays:* Jeanroy emends to *ni·ls enfrays*, following DIKa.
    16. *escas:* Jeanroy prints *escars*.
    18. Jeanroy adopts ADIK's *los deya* for Ca's *lo deya*.
    19. *Ist trobador:* We follow Jeanroy in rejecting C's unique reading *Li t.* in favor of all other MSS.
    23. *donas, em pantays:* Jeanroy prints *dompnas, en pantays*.
    24. Jeanroy prints *cui* for *cuy*; also, he lists A's reading as *mout volon escoutar*, but the MS reads *mout vol hom*.
    28. *Escassedatz:* Jeanroy prints *Escarsetatz*.
    29. *din:* Jeanroy prints *dinz*; also, he lists *delbajs* as C's reading, but the MS reads *de bays*; he emends to *d'Abays*, following a. *bais* means "kiss," and is not attested meaning "low"; we have thus followed Jeanroy in adopting a's reading.
    30. *layssa, yssir:* Jeanroy prints *laissa, issir*.
    31. *vey, fallir:* Jeanroy prints *vei, faillir*.
    35. *que Dieus:* Jeanroy prints *qui Dieus*.
    36. *e totz vius:* Jeanroy emends this to *o totz vius*.
    37. Dejeanne suggested emending *ni cobrir* to *ni·ns cobrir*.
    44. *que son:* Jeanroy emends this to *qu'en son*.

49-56. We have reversed the order of tornadas as they exist in a, suggested by the rhyme-scheme: abcb of stanza 9 mirrors the abcb of each stanza's first quatrain; caca mirrors, with an important metrical repetition characteristic of final lines (cf. the tornada of Song 3), each stanza's last couplet.
    49. Jeanroy does not list a's reading *Fagz el*.
    53. *diz:* Jeanroy prints *dis*; he also corrects *qe* to *qi*.
    56. Jeanroy emends *no·n pot hom* to *be·n pot hom*, but refrains from translating the result.

GLOSSARY OF SPECIAL WORDS

The meanings given in the Glossary are only those reflected in the texts of Cercamon. Some of the listed words may have additional meanings in other contexts which are not given in this Glossary. "TN" means the word is discussed in the Textual Notes; "fn" means the word is mentioned in the footnotes to the translation.

ADES   1st sing. pres. ind. of *adesar*, to reach, get close to   7.6
AFIC (VER)   engagement; *ver afic*, the Last Judgment   1.29 (TN)
AIZIU (S')   3rd sing. pres. subj. of *s'aizivar*, to find welcome with   1.35 (TN)
BIAYS (EN)   obliquely, hence deviously   8.21
CREIS (LO)   offspring   1.39 (TN)
DESPLEI   3rd sing. pres. subj. of *despleiar*, to present, perform   6.36
DEVES   prohibition; area that is off-limits   3.48
DRUDEJAN   possibly 3rd plur. pres. ind. of **drudejar*, to court; also possibly a verbal noun   7.17 (TN)
ENAURADA   mad, giddy, out of one's mind   4.14
ENCOR   1st sing. pres. ind. of *encorre*, to incur, contract   7.38 (TN)
ESCASSEDATZ   stinginess, tightfistedness   8.28
ESTORT   past part. of *estorser*, to deliver, save   1.47
FORT (PER)   of necessity   2.7 (fn)
FURMIR   to deliver a message to, get through to   4.44
GUAZALHA   (business) engagement   2.15
INTRATZ, INTRADAS   past part. of *intrar*, to begin   1.48, 8.23 (fn)
MAÏSTRE   trained professional of a certain status, e.g. a craftsman or a musician   2.10, 28, 32, 37, 41, 46, 50
MALVESTATZ   baseness, badness, degeneracy   1.5 (fn), 7.12, 8.30
SIRVEN   man of intermediate status, under wage, in a minor supervisory position   8.25 (Life of the Author)
SOUDADIERS   man under wage for, e.g., military or entertainment purposes; mercenary   8.33 (Life of the Author)
TRISTAN   participial adj. formed on **tristar*, to be sad, have a heavy heart   7.38
UZAN   pres. part. of *uzar*, to practise   6.34 (TN)

INDEX OF NAMES

ADAM   see Genesis 1 1.21
ANFOS (N')   Alfonso VII of Castille; or possibly Alphonse-
   Jourdain of Toulouse 1.36 (fn; Life of the Author)
ARAGO   Aragon 1.52
AUNIS   region in France southwest of Poitiers 1.48 (TN)
BARRAU (LI)   the people of Bar in France 1.9 (TN)
CERCA(L)MON(T,Z)   the poet 1.50, 3.57, 8.53
DEUS   God 1.19, 45, 47, 2.10, 3.23, 4.11, 43, 6.16, 7.39,
   8.35, 38, 42
EBLO (')   probably Ebles II of Ventadorn 1.50 (Life of the
   Author)
ENGOLMES   the people of the Angoumois 1.44
ESPAIGN'   Spain 1.52
FRANCES   the inhabitants of the Capetian domain 1.37 (TN)
FRANSA   the Capetian domain 2.33 (TN)
GASCO (LI)   the Gascons 1.31, 51
GUILHALMI   the poet's companion 2.19, 30, 35, 39, 44, 48
   53
JACME (SANT)   St. James 1.53 (fn)
JOAN (SAINT)   St. John 6.16
JUDAS   Judas 8.35
LIMOZI   the people of the Limousin 1.44 (TN)
NICOLAU (SAIN)   St. Nicholas 7.52
NORMAN   the Normans 1.37
PANTACOSTA   Pentecost, Whitsun 2.51
PEITAVIS (LO)   William, Xth Duke of Aquitaine, VIIIth Count
   of Poitiers 1.6
PEITAU   Poitou 1.8
P(E)ITIEU(S)   Poitiers; the *coms de P(e)itieus* is William X
   in 1.13, and Louis VII in 2.18
ROAYS   Edessa 8.45 (see Life of the Author)
SALVADOR (SAINT)   Christ, the Holy Savior; or possibly Saint
   Savior, a place name 7.43 (see Life of the Author)
SEGNERS   the Lord 1.17
SERRAZIS   Saracens 1.42

INDEX OF OPENING LINES

                                                              Poem No.

Ab lo pascor m'es bel q'eu chant	7
Ab lo temps qe·s fai refreschar	4
Assatz es ora oimai q'eu chant	6
Car vei fenir a tot dia	2
Lo plaing comenz iradamen	1
Per fin'amor m'esjauzira	5
Pus nostre temps comens'a brunezir	8
Qant la douch'aura s'amarcis	3

Manuscript a, pages 364–70
(Courtesy of the d'Este Library, Modena)

e iois iouenz sailla son cuipatz a penna mala qui ques crida foc
e flama. uia dinz e sia preza degollem ioi e iouen e preza sia
aucira.

Ali segnor con es grans tala si morsen fill o seng failla reteigna
p merauillia. lo bec o longla o lala. q de paut auures gran rami
qn bona pugna es mira. p qe nesp en ater la flor apel la cenza
e pont roba finni pusa
Non uoil far paraula longua pza es la francha causa sis met
enrecluzogna. chascus la fier e de rami e las denz li frango bien
copa mi enaps d'argen. mantel e noi troba mais un paren de pa ... en
mira.
Ben crei sens mensonga. than primer hypocha clau qil fan
pear copar ses faiuer sogna. tante on ges qe il la tisma. per q en
de paut for gran nausa copani enaps durgen mantel uare ni pena gei pi

Maritz q l'auteui con grata. pot ben sabre q seus pega e mostra
qe hom li mesera. p ab eis so fuit lo sala. e fai i tort si sen clama
q ben egal d'uira. qt qi cue compra cue uen ar sego la lei d' pza

Di qi nais la uos barata. nic uiu morz q deu descresen. cui no
fai solatz ni recra no sia la segna plata. cel qi sa mais na clo toma
ces uest la blanca camira. e fai son segnor suffren e te si cons a sagues

Alegret fas es en dis guiza ewas far clau sualen mi de gonela
camira.

Circ amonz

Quan la douz aura sa marzis. eil fueilla chai desus uerian. eil
auzel chanzon lur laks. q ieu de sospir e de chan damor qe m te
lassat eps qeu anc nom agitz em poder.

Res qe eu clamor non ai conqis mas con lo trebail. el afan ni yes ta ni
grieus nos conuerts

Per una ioia mes baudis. fina cant non amei tan. can totz los gentz
brunezis. de lai enuill. e si resplan dieu preiarai qenqer laiq o qe
la ueian ou iazer.

Totz treuail ebram e freims. p samor dormen e ueillam tol paor
ai qe mes faillis. no maus pensar con lo deman. nicu seruir lei dos
anz o tres. e pueis ben leu sabran lo uer.

Non muer ni uia ni non gueris ni mal nom sen. e si fai gran
car de samor non soi deuis. ni ia sauvai ni can. qer leis es tota la
merces qer pot sorzer o dechaier.

Bel mes cant el ma fallatis em fai bacler en nau muzan. de leis
mes bel. si mescaremis om gaba deleis o denan. capres lo mal me
uenral bes. ben lieu sa leis uen a plazer.

Sela nom uol ualgra muris. lo dia qem pres en coman. ai las tan
souet maucis. can del sieu amor mi fes semblan. qe torna ma en
tal deues. qe nuil autra non uoil uezer.

Totz cossiros men esiauzis. car sieu la dopti e la blan. p leis sentir
o fals o fis. o drechuriers o plen denjan. o totz uilas o totz cortes. o trebaillos
o de lezer.

Mas cui qe plassa o cui qe pes. e lam pot sil uol enreqir.

Sercamons

Assatz es ora oi mai qeu chant. tant ai estat a condusomitz. canc
mes chanz non fon lueing. auzitz. mas eram uau ia ueueillant e
irei mon ioi recobran contre l'iuern. el freig auro.

De ioi nom cal enan. canc un saliorn. non fui garmiz. e sui mal coi
prior so ditz. si qen tres sens. uau sospiran lo leziriez cui damor
gran mi dozm ni ueil. ni aug ni liei.

Sanc p̄ amor. anc i ueilham. nin fui anc fols ni trassuitz. ni
coniliatz p̄ chamjaritz. eran lau dieu e saint ioan. cab tal amor
nan amoran. canc nom chanies p̄ autra mei.

Cesta non cug qe iam sieu ia de leis. no soigauentz ni non ssi
gauentz tant asolatitz. qe ia veil qeira mil deman. petit ni pro
mi tan mi qant. ni mal ni be. ni re mi qei.

Tant la sei coinda e prezan. el saigz de leis estant es litz qe sai.
me fenc p̄ engenritz. e lai a hiu la coman. la nug el iorn. el mes el
an. caissi soi sieus con esser dei.

Plas es lo ueis nauc lafinan ses ___ ui la fals apostitz. e estotz.
en aissi noviz. cap motz politz. lo ___ uzan. e tot ades uas mei
lluxam ses qi bel chant ni bel desplei.

sercamons.

Ab lo temps qes fai refreschar. lo segle ereuidezir ueil un no
uel chant comenzar. dun amor cui am e dezir. mas tant ses de
mi soignada qieu non la puesc acoseguir. ni de mos digz
no sagracia.

Ja mai res nom pot conortar. abanz mi laissaraz morir. can
man fag de mi donz sobrar. lauzeniador. cui deus azir. las tan
l'aurai dezirada. qe p̄ lei plaing. plor e sospir. e vau cum
res en aurada.

Aqesta don mauzes chantar es plus bella qieu no sai dir. tam
es fina e smerada e ____ ____ ____ ____ fresta calbe e bel
____ ___ blancha ses brunezir. qe e non es uexuiada. ni om de
____ ___ seis non pot mal dir. tant es fina esmerada e sobre
totas deu prezar.

De dire ner segon mon albir. den segnamen e de paular. cancon uole
son amic trair. e ieu sols la uegada. cue cresei uengen nuesclis. ni sis-
so don sospirada.

Anc ieu de lei non uole clamar. ger sus uol me pot iauzir. e
a ben portar de donar. da ço on me pot enquerir. no pot sa lonia
durada. gel mariar en port. el dormir. cue no mes plus agirrada.

Amors es douça al mirar. e amara al departir. gen un iouen uos
fara plorar. e autre iogar. e beuedir. gen sai damor enseigniada.
on plus la cuidaua seruir. plhes ia mi cambiada.

Messaiges. uai si deus ti guar. e sapchas ab mi donz sufrir. gen
non puesc lomamen estar. sai ius ni de lai querir. si costa mi
despoliada. non la puesc baizar e tenir. dinz cambra encortinada.

Sercamon.

Ab lo pascor mes bel gen chant. en estiu al eniran de mai. can par
la flors sobrels uerchant. e son reuerdezit li gai. mout mi ual
paur lo temps cors es. gen non ai ioi ni non la des ni de sa comp-
compagnia non sau.

Per ge damor an abestan. li malvas enoios saurai. con li meillor.
el plus pregan iouenz. e saig fraing. e dechai. e maluestatz a son
luer. ges en amistatz. car ueis non es amatz ni damiga. nos iau.

Ben sai ge lor es mal estan. als molleiratz. car se san gui dom
neiador. ni drudeiar. ni es quizardos ge lor nes chai ditz. el reprocher lo paies. gi glazi fai a glazi es feritz. de is lo seu colp mortau.
fals amador al meu semblan. uostrer lo danz. e non pueis mai de
gran dolor. es acordan. con lus lautre galitciai. e pos nos aves en ges
deut molheirat. marit. tug tres sias del perhat comunau -

368 Siuer maior seretz arden. al uizizi del derrer plai. engein
dor sil destriau. en la pena qe non tresuai. on sera tortz lo
mals el bes. iutiatz e nom clam mercey donna caia deus des le iau.

Non a ualor daissi enan. cela cabtos ni ab tresiai. p aisenger lo
cor trystan. qe cheus tan felsa non fetz sai. miels li fora ia no mes
ges. enanz qe faillimentz fes. don er parlat tro en peisau.

Saint saluaire soi malbec qan lai el regne on mi donz estau.
ab la genser si qen baizan si en nostre couen uerai. e rem do
zo qe ma promes. pueys al iorn ston ira congs si be les mal
al qe los breau.

Amics dignas lim can bues. si passal terme qauem pres.
qieu soi motz p soin nicolau.

Sercamonz

Pos nostre temps comensa brunezir. e linueria son de la foilla
  e de
bla   soleil. uei tan baissar lo fraig. per qeil iorn son scur
e tenebros. e hom non au dauzel ni chant ni lais p ioi clamor
nos deu om esbaudir.

A qestamor non pot hom tan seruir qe mil aitan noil closses qui
iardos. qe pretz e iois erant qant es enaiss nauuan aicel qi seruen pote
uos. qanc non passet couinent mi esfraiss mais p semblan gren esa cogeret.

P er leis deu hom esperar. e sofrir tan es sos pretz ualenz e cabalos.
tanc non ai soin dels amadors sauais de ric estais ni paupre orgoillos.
qe plus de mil non a uns tan uerais qe si namors lo clea obezir.

A si trobador entreue ce mentir. assollin chautz e moilletz e spos
e uar chzen qamoys tornem brais p qe ler deuen on gelos e donnos son
entraiat en partrais. car trop uolon escoutar e auzir.

Cist serue salsson a plusors gegir. pretz e iouen e donar ades tros.
e qe proeza non cug sia mais. qe cauze fatz tan las claus dels baros.
n aint na serrat dinz la ciutat da bais don maluestatz no laisa un issir

Certamenz diz qe uos amors si eras. merauill es com pot l irea suffrir. q la
damor es paors q es glais. e non pot hom trap viure ni munr.

fagz el lo uex e non deu ueillezir. segon aisso qe monstra la razgz qans
bonanous. non galbet ni frons anz ama ioialsarcy amoros.

Sercamonz.

Lo plaing comenz iradamen. dun uers don hai lo cor dolen
ire dolor e marriment. ai cor uei abaissar iouenz. maluestatz puei e
iois disen. des pois muric lo peitauis.

Remazut son li pretz gillau qi salon idir de peitau. ai com lo plain li
barrau. e sa longa sai estau. segners lo baro qieu mentau met et
sius platz empauadis.

Del comte de pitieu mi plaing. qera de proeza compaing. des pos
pretz e donars sostraing peiam sa lonias sai remaing. segners
de seren. lo seuitz estraing. qe molt p son gensa sa sis.

Glorios dieus a uos me clam. cor mi zoletz aqll qieu am aisi
com uos formetz adam. lo defendetz. del felliam. del foc de fern
qe non laflam. q qest segles. nos es charnis.

A qest segle foing p emic. qel paubres non aten ni ric. ai con son
uan fuit mei amic. e sai remanon fuit mendic pero sui ben gal
uest a sic. seran li mal dals bos deuis.

Gasto cortes nominatiu. p dut aues lo segnoriu. ser uos deu etze p si q
don iouenz se clama. chaitiu. que us non troba on saiziu. mas qan
nan fos. qa ioi con qis.

Plagnen lo normans e frances. e lieu lo be plagnee lo reis.
cui laisset la terra el creis. pos tan grant honor li creis mal estera.
si non pareis. chi vouge sobre sevrezis.

S qil uan iora. cui qe pes. de si mort e de ngalmes. si el uisqes. ni
deu plagues. el los agra de se conges. estort en son cor dieus lo pres.
el dos nes intratz en aunis.

Jo plaingz. es de bona ragio. qe cercamors trametneo lo ai.
com la plaigno li gasco. cil de pain e d'arago. sainz racine
membratz del baro. qe deuant uos iai pelegris.

Encadenetz.

C amjada ses mauentura. don ieu nu sofeira estatz. e s'embreu
non meillura. serai amics desamatz. qeram soignha de sa amia
cela qem solia traire. mas changos e mos gaissos. e ma nzes.
mes sailida. si eu voil for changso graziria. qes mes aiuda
desen. e non chantavai plazen.

Si eu p ma sofrsaitura. pros domna soi malmenatz. e suplei
tot cant hom iura. qeu fora desesperatz. mas eu son leiat no nai
qe anc pros domna qe los nom fer laissar ses failida. son amic
mas lai seruida. de som poder. franchamen. e sieu no leta gen.

D ompna nous met en vancura. neguna vem qem fazatz.
anz aurai tant de mezura. qem sofeirai tot em pes p lo ses qem
soletz faire. po greu mera retraire. qe uos uostras faitz
desmentatz a uostra uida. ce ex me bo lo seus oblida qe no assatz
faillimont q̄l plaing mai qel dan qi pren.

Dompna se gaires peiura. uesmi uostra uoluntatz. e no
uoletz auer. cura tan euci mai me retengn hatz.

Frontispiece of de Lantier's "Geoffroy Rudel, ou le Troubadour" (1825). (Courtesy of the University of Rochester Library)

The Poetry of
Jaufre Rudel

Illumination heading Jaufre's poems in Manuscript I, B.N. fr. 854, fol. 121v, depicting the poet dying in the arms of the Countess of Tripoli. (Courtesy of the Bibliothèque Nationale)

Introduction

Life of the Author

Jaufre Rudel is one of the best known of the Old Provençal troubadours, who wrote in the south of France in the twelfth and thirteenth centuries. Yet we know little about this lord of Blaye, who lived in the second quarter of the twelfth century. More than his lyrics, it is the legend of his distant love that has inspired authors as varied as Petrarch, Stendhal, Rostand, Browning, Heine, Carducci, and their readers in turn. According to his thirteenth-century biography or *vida* (version of Manuscripts AB):

> Jaufre Rudel, Prince of Blaye, was a very noble man. And he fell in love with the Countess of Tripoli, without having seen her, because of the great goodness and courtliness which he heard tell of her from the pilgrims who came from Antioch. And he wrote many good songs about her, with good melodies and poor words. And because of his desire, he took the cross and set sail to go see her. But in the ship he fell very ill, to the point where those who were with him thought he was dead. However, they got him—a dead man, as they thought—to Tripoli, to an inn. And it was made known to the Countess, and she came to his bedside, and took him in her arms. And he knew she was the Countess, and recovered sight [MSS. IK: hearing] and smell, and praised God because He had kept him alive until he had seen her. And so he died in the arms of the lady. And she had him buried with honor in the Temple at Tripoli. Then, the same day, she became a nun because of the grief which she felt for him and for his death.

> Jaufres Rudels de Blaia si fo molt gentils hom, princes de Blaia. Et enamoret se de la comtessa de Tripol, ses vezer, per lo gran ben e per la gran cortesia qu'el auzi dir de lieis als pelegrins que vengron d'Antiocha. E fetz de lieis mains bons vers ab bons sons [et] ab paubres motz. E per volontat de lieis vezer, el se crozet e

mes se en mar, per anar lieis vezer. Et adoncs en la nau lo pres mout grans malautia, si que cill qui eron ab lui cuideron q'el fos mortz en la nau. Mas tant feiron q'il lo conduisseron a Tripol, en un alberc, aissi cum per mort. E fo faich a saber a la comtessa, et adoncs ella s'en venc a lui, al sieu lieich, e pres lo entre sos bratz. Et el saup que so era la comtessa, si recobret lo vezer e·l flazar, e lauzet Dieu e·l grazi que l'avia la vida sostenguda tro qu'el l'agues vista; et enaissi el moric entre·ls braz de la dompna. Et ella lo fetz honradamenz sepeillir en la maison del Temple de Tripol; e pois, en aquel meteus dia, ela se rendet monga, per la dolor que ella ac de lui e de la soa mort.

This account, retold in every century since Jaufre's, fits in to some degree with what we can infer historically about the poet. We know that Jaufre Rudel was, as the *vida* claims, one of a line of lords (*princes*) who held land roughly within the square of territory formed by Saintes, Angoulême, Bergerac, and Bordeaux in the southwest of France. Just north of Bordeaux is the castle of Blaye, built on an escarpment dominating the Garonne River on its right bank. Because of its link to Roland, the Carolingian hero of Roncevaux, Blaye was a popular site on the pilgrimage route to the shrine of St. James at Compostela in northern Spain. However, little remains of the medieval citadel built, according to at least one legend, over Roland's tomb.

Since the end of the tenth century the troubadour's ancestors had held Blaye (according to Cravayat; see Select Bibliography for all sources). The first of them to be named Jaufre Rudel did homage both to his cousins, the Counts of Angoulême, and to his overlords, the Counts of Poitiers, late in the eleventh century. Over succeeding generations the House of Blaye was periodically at war with the Houses of Angoulême or Poitiers, or both. In the twelfth century the first known troubadour, William, VII Count of Poitiers, IX Duke of Aquitaine, seized the castle from Girard of Blaye and destroyed its walls and dungeon, as we are told in the anonymous *History of the Bishops and Counts of Angoulême* (ed. J. Boussard, p. 33). It was not until the time of Count William's son, William VIII (d. 1137), mourned by Cercamon in his *Lo plaing comenz*, that Blaye was recaptured and rebuilt by Wulgrin II, Count of Angoulême, and restored to his vassal Girard or Girard's son, the troubadour Jaufre Rudel.

Introduction

We learn from the Cartulary of the Priory of Sainte Gemme (Cravayat) that Jaufre succeeded to his father's title and castle. Although the original charter has been lost, a late seventeenth-century transcription tells us that it was Jaufre Rudel who at an undetermined date fulfilled some of his late father's obligations toward the priory. With the earlier document signed by Jaufre, his brother, and his father, this is the only historical evidence by which we can identify a Jaufre Rudel, lord of Blaye (*dominus Blaviae*) in the second quarter of the twelfth century. It should be mentioned, however, that there are also later descendants named Jaufre Rudel attested as lords of Blaye until almost the middle of the fourteenth century (see the article of P. Julien-Laferrière). Early scholars sought to identify the poet with one of these descendants, but Jaufre has since been restored to his proper period.

The first historical reference to the poet Jaufre Rudel is by the troubadour Marcabru, who sends one of his songs encouraging the French crusaders "to Lord Jaufre Rudel overseas." There is no reason to doubt that his dedicatee is the Jaufre Rudel we have described, and that Jaufre took the cross to participate in the Second Crusade, as his *vida* relates. That Jaufre went on crusade is further supported by what we know of the men with whom Jaufre was in contact, three, possibly four, of whom he refers to in his poems.

One of the poet's references is to his "Good Protector" (5.33), and suggests William VI Taillefer, Count of Angoulême (1140–79), Jaufre's cousin and suzerain. In the passage mentioned, Jaufre may be interpreted as implying that it is thanks to his "Good Protector" that he is able to go on crusade. William VI embarked with Alphonse-Jourdain of Toulouse from Port-de-Bou in the summer of 1147, made stops in Sicily and at Constantinople, and landed at St. John of Acre in the Holy Land on April 13, 1148. Cravayat believes that Jaufre sailed with William and Alphonse, and the nature of the Crusade also suggests that this is so, since both the French and German armies departed as a relative whole in the summer of 1147. Louis VII's army left about a month after that of Conrad III. The contingent that went by sea left still later, since the sea journey was shorter. As Lavisse, for example, mentions (*Histoire de France*, III, 13–17), the Second Crusade was not, as the First had been, characterized by small groups setting out on their own; it is likely that all followed the great armies in the summer of 1147. Some, among whom was Jaufre's friend Hugh VII of Lusignan (mentioned in 4.32), went with the kings by land; others, such as William VI and Alphonse-Jourdain, sailed. But all departed as a unified crusading army. Thus it is likely, if Jaufre took the cross, that he did so at this time. And if there is any truth to the *vida*, then the chances are that Jaufre went with his suzerain, William VI.

Two other figures to whom Jaufre refers in his poems are traditionally taken to be Alphonse-Jourdain of Toulouse and his bastard son Bertrand, who went with his father on crusade. In *No sap chantar* (No. 3), Jaufre says that he wishes Lord Bertrand in Quercy and the Count in Toulouse to hear his song and that "they will do something there that people will sing about." Some scholars have thought that "there" in this quotation refers to the Holy Land. But it is perhaps more reasonable to assume that "there" refers to where Bertrand and Alphonse are at the time. If so, this suggests a date for *No sap chantar* prior to the summer of 1147 when Alphonse and Bertrand left for the East.

A final reference by Jaufre is to *Hugon Brun*, or Hugh the Swarthy, VII Count of Lusignan and of the Marche, who, as mentioned, departed with Louis VII's army in June of 1147. Of Hugh, Jaufre says that "the men of Poitou, the men of Berry, the men of Guyenne, and the Bretons rejoice for him" (4.33–35). If Jaufre did indeed leave on crusade by a separate route from Hugh, then this may be a kind of farewell and a well-wishing to his friend. If so, then this song, *Quan lo rius*, was written close to the summer of 1147, along with No. 5, *Quan lo rossinhols*, which exhorts the worthy to depart for Bethlehem.

As for the remaining historicity of the *vida*, it is just possible that Jaufre was known to his contemporaries as a man who had fallen in love with the Countess of Tripoli, whom he had never seen but about whom all had no doubt heard. The Countess of Tripoli at the time was Hodierna of Jerusalem, and her husband, Count Raymond II, was known to be so jealous of her as to keep her "in a state of Oriental seclusion" (Runciman, II, 332–33). Such a situation could easily have given rise to pilgrims' stories.

Marcabru's reference suggests strongly that Jaufre did go on crusade. Some of Jaufre's songs make it clear that he was interested in a distant love though the precise nature of this love is not clear. There is no historical evidence that he was buried in the Temple at

The Rudel castle as it appears today. (Photo G. Wolf)

An engraving of Tripoli printed in Runciman's *History of the Crusades*, from *Syria, Illustrated*, vol. III by Bartlett, Allon, etc., London, 1838. (Courtesy of the New York Public Library)

Tripoli. That he reached Tripoli at all and saw the Countess has been, and will be, a matter for conjecture.

Artistic Achievement

One of Jaufre's achievements is to have become a legend by creating the theme of a "distant love"; and yet the nature of this distant love has never been defined. Critics have not yet resolved whether Jaufre really fell in love with a distant lady and wrote about it biographically, whether he was preaching philosophically on an abstract theme, or whether the idea of a distant love was a fiction in the poet's mind, perhaps designed at the outset to baffle the curious.

Jaufre created a lucid style, and his poems are easily read. As pointed out by Jeanroy, his versification is simple also. His poems are composed of between five and eight full stanzas, of six to eight lines each. Each line contains seven or eight syllables, and masculine (final-syllable stressed) lines predominate. Again as noted by Jeanroy, a peculiar trait of Jaufre is his use of rhymes repeated not within stanzas but once in each successive stanza; these are called *rimas esparsas*. A famous example of this is the word *loing* in No. 6. Usually Jaufre employs the same rhymes in all stanzas, but he varies this in two songs (2 and 4) in which pairs of stanzas with identical rhymes alternate with pairs of stanzas with the same rhymes shifted. A final point made by Jeanroy is the frequency in Jaufre of rhyme words which are used more than once in one song.

An aspect of Jaufre's poems that deserves attention is a point of style which he shares with the "second generation" of troubadour poets, and to some degree with William IX as well. This is a preoccupation with love as a theme, rather than with the theme of the lady, which is given prominence by later poets. The earlier troubadours tend to discourse on love; the lady is almost secondary. It is curious that in Jaufre's poems not once do we find the word *domna*. Instead we have *elha* or *leis* (she) and abstractions. Although in Jaufre and in the other earlier poets there is little doubt that, at least at times, the act of love was their subject matter, it is still the idea of love and its ethic, rather than the lady, which is the focus of attention.

It is remarkable that Jaufre's simple style, which conveys an air of detachment and at times almost of mysticism, was little imitated.

There are one or two passages in Cercamon which recall Jaufre's poems, but it is not certain that these are cases of influence. Jaufre shares his individuality to some degree with William: the tale of nocturnal embarrassment (No. 2) shows the influence of William's bawdy poems, which tell "what went on." But for the most part Jaufre, like William, stands stylistically alone. Only his legend was celebrated by later poets, while Jaufre the poet became a model of the faithful lover.

Finally, Jaufre, like Cercamon in one or two poems, strikes a balance between dream and reality, between business and pleasure, which allows us to place his elusive poems firmly in the historical context of the mid-twelfth century. This dichotomy in itself gives an insight into the values of a vernacular poet writing between the First and Second Crusades. Jaufre took part in the events and politics of his time, but he saw these commitments as linked to the life of the spirit, which entailed artistic creation, moral teaching, and the improvement of daily living. All of these aspects are present in his poems.

Sources and Influences

Like Cercamon, Jaufre makes use of classical themes acquired through twelfth-century channels. Once again, reminiscences of Ovid are particularly noticeable, since the Roman poet's vogue was at its height during this period. We find echoes of Ovidian scenes, such as that in *Amores* 2.2.5–8, where a girl replies *non licet* (it is not permitted) to the poet's urgent request for a meeting. In Jaufre 1.45–48 the lady comes to the poet and says that she cannot meet him now because "jealous boors" have started a dispute which will make it difficult for them to enjoy themselves. In *Amores* 3.11a, Ovid speaks of the burden of *turpis amor* which he has borne too long. Jaufre in No. 2 speaks of the "foolish burden" which he has now cast off. In Ovid we find love as a flame (*Am.* 1.2, etc.). Jaufre says that he is not surprised if he is "aflame" with love (4.16). Even "joy" is found in Ovid (*Veneris gaudia, Am.* 2.3.2; *mea gaudia, Am.,* 2.5.29, etc.). In some ways Ovid seems to be everywhere, to suffuse the medieval genre. But he can be identified only occasionally; and the *joi* found in the early troubadours, especially in Jaufre, reflects contemporary as well as Ovidian influences.

There are few borrowings of any consequence between Jaufre

and his contemporaries. Three examples of them reveal perhaps only a common poetic diction:

vezem . . . *rius e fontanas esclarzir* (William, 7.1–3) We see . . . streams and fountains shine	Quan lo *rius* de la *fontana* s'esclarzis . . . (Jaufre, 4.1–2) When the fountain's flow shines . . .
qu'enaissi *fuy* de nueits *fadatz* sobr'un puej au (W. 4.11–12) for I was thus enchanted at night on a high hill	qu'enaissi·*m fadet* mos pairis (J.R. 6.48) for thus my godfather fixed my fate
ben dey, si puesc, *al mielhs* anar (W. 9.4) I must, if I can, go to the best	vau *mo mielhs* queren (J.R. 5.30) I seek what is best for me

Two more passages also raise the question of influence:

metge querrai al meu albir e non sai cau; bos *metges* er si·*m pot guerir* (W. 4.21–23) I think I shall seek a doctor and I don't know which; he'll be a good doctor if he can cure me	e d'aquest mal *mi pot guerir* ses gart de *metge* sapien (J.R. 1.55–56) and she can cure me of this pain without the help of a learned doctor

As for Jaufre's influence on later poets, it was the legend rather than the poems which found good fortune. Jaufre was an individualist, and he seems, in contrast to a poet such as Marcabru, to have had no followers in his themes. He was no doubt familiar with the songs of his contemporaries as common words and phrases show, but he stands as a lone figure among the early troubadours. However, his songs were well known, and in addition to a broad representation in the songbooks, including the music of four of his six songs (see Musical Appendix), later poets reproduced the meter and rhyme-scheme (though not rhymes) of Poem 2 (six times), of Poem 6 (four times), of Poem 3 (seven times); and Peire Cardenal copied the meter and rhymes of Poem 5 exactly. Jaufre is also quoted in the French romance *Guillaume de Dôle* (line 1299), and in the *Breviari d'Amor* (lines 29417–22, ed. Ricketts), a didactic poem by the fourteenth-century Franciscan Matfre Ermengau.

The fame of the Jaufre legend can be seen in two poetic debates of the later troubadour period. The first, which is found in Mahn's *Gedichte der Troubadours*, III, 169, is a *partimen* between Izarn and Rofian, dated by Blum after 1240. Rofian asks Izarn if he would rather have his lady once in a hidden place and then die or love her unrequited. Izarn answers that he would prefer the second, to love his lady without reward rather than die after one *joi*. Rofian accuses Izarn of loving disloyally, and cites Jaufre as an example:

> I shall know why you pretend to be so pained,
> because you are so changeable and deceitful with respect to love;
> you are scarcely like the worthy viscount
> Jaufre Rudel, who died on the journey . . .
>
> sabrai per qe·us feinhetz tan doloros,
> pos qe d'amor est tan var ni ginhos;
> non sembles ges lo vesconte valen
> Jaufre Rudel qe moric al passage . . .

Izarn replies that Jaufre did not make the voyage for *joi*:

> for you know if the amorous viscount
> Jaufre could endure death and suffering;
> it wasn't for any joy that he made that voyage.
>
> qar vos sabes si·l vescoms amoros
> Jaufres saupes penre mort ni turmen:
> non es nuills jois per q'el fes cell viage.

Rofian rejoins that Jaufre did die in desire for his lady, and it is for this that we praise him.

The second poem, a *tenso* between Giraut de Salignac and Peironet (Riquer, III, 788–90), was written probably around 1300. In it, Giraut asks, "Which better maintains love, the heart or the eyes of the man who truly loves his lady?" Peironet argues for the eyes, and Girart for the heart. Peironet cites the example of Andrieu de France, and Girart that of Jaufre:

> for the love of the eyes is worthless if the heart does not feel,
> and [yet] without the eyes the heart can sincerely
> love her whom it has in fact never seen,
> as did Jaufre his beloved.
>
> c'amor dels hueills non val se·l cor non sen,
> e ses los hueills pot lo cor francamen

> amar sella c'anc non vi a prezen,
> si com Jaufre Rudel fetz de s'amia.

Jaufre is also mentioned by the Catalan troubadour Guiraut de Cabrera in his famous *ensenhamen* (instruction poem), *Cabra joglar*, which Pirot has dated before 1162.

The later troubadours took their poetry and their tradition to Italy. The early Italian humanists knew these poets well. Petrarch's often-quoted line attests to the fame of the legend in the Middle Ages:

> Jaufre Rudel who used the sail and oar
> to seek his death
>
> Giaufre Rudel ch'usò la vela e'l remo
> a cercar la sua morte   (*Trionfo d'Amore*, IV, 52)

There is mention of Jaufre in Mario Equicola's *Libro di natura d'amore* (Venice, 1525), in the *De pulchro et de amore* of Agostino Nifo (Rome, 1529), and by Petrarch's commentators Alessandro Vellutello (1525) and Giovanni Gesualdo (1531). The most famous and elaborate treatment of Jaufre occurs in Jehan de Nostredame's extravagant *Vies des plus célèbres et anciens poètes provençaux* (1575), whose sources, if not wholly imaginary, are not known (for references, see Vincenti).

After the Renaissance, what was known of Jaufre was handed down in the books of the scholars and antiquarians Barbieri, Crescimbeni, Bastero, and Ste. Palaye. From this point the legend diverged to become part of the stock of nineteenth-century scholarship and a source of romantic subject matter for poets.

One of the first of these poets was Ludwig Uhland, who, through Crescimbeni's translation, used Nostredame as a source for his *Sängerliebe* (1812–14), which Carducci later described as "reminiscent of stale leftovers" ("transpira un sentore di stantio riscaldato"). Another German lyricist who was inspired by Jaufre's legend was Vogl, in whose ballad "Melisunde" the theme was revived. Better known is Heine's "Geoffroy Rudel und Melisende von Tripoli" in the first book ("Historien") of his *Romanzero*. In Heine's version of the legend, the princess, out of grief, instead of entering holy orders, weaves the love story into a tapestry. The ghosts of the dead lovers come out of the tapestry and live out their love:

> "Melisende! Bliss and blossom!
> When I look into your eyes,
> I live again—dead is only
> My mortal woe and sorrow!"
>
> "Jaufre! We loved each other
> Once in a dream, and now below
> We love each other even in death—
> The god of Love performed this miracle!"
>
> "Melisende! Glück und Blume!
> Wenn ich dir ins Auge sehe,
> Leb ich auf—gestorben ist
> Nur mein Erdenleid und -wehe!"
>
> "Geoffroy! Wir liebten uns
> Einst im Traume, und jetztunder
> Lieben wir uns gar im Tode—
> Gott Amour tat dieses Wunder!"

In England, Robert Browning used the Jaufre legend in his "Rudel to the Lady of Tripoli," one of the later poems of *Men and Women*. In this poem, Rudel has chosen as his device the sunflower, and this flower is symbolic of the poet's songs. Bees swarm to the flower as men to songs, but the flower cares only for the sun toward which it turns. Similarly for Jaufre, who, heedless of men's acclaim, turns only toward the East:

> —Say, men feed
> On songs I sing, and therefore bask the bees
> On my flower's breast as on a platform broad:
> But as the flower's concern is not for these
> But solely for the sun, so men applaud
> In vain this Rudel, he not looking here
> But to the East—the East! Go, say this, Pilgrim dear!"

Swinburne took up the theme briefly in his poem "The Triumph of Time," which treats of unfulfilled love. Jaufre serves Swinburne well here, and appears toward the end of the poem as "a singer of France of old." At the end of the century A. Mary Robinson added her voice to the legend in "Rudel and the Lady of Tripoli" (*The Collected Poems*, London, 1902, p. 294).

In France, "Geoffroy Rudel, ou Le Troubadour. Poème en Huit Chants" was printed by M. de Lantier in Paris in 1825. But

Introduction

Rostand's *La princesse lointaine* is perhaps the best known of the nineteenth-century versions of the Jaufre legend. The whole play is devoted to the enacting of the *vida*. Rostand, following Nostredame, adds that Jaufre is accompanied on the journey by the troubadour Bertran d'Alamanon, who is charged upon arrival with being messenger to the princess. Bertran falls in love with her, and she almost falls in love with him; however, she sees the error of her escape from duty and in the end remains faithful to the *vida*, leaving Bertran an intruder.

Carducci spanned the poetic and scholarly traditions in poem and essay. He traces the history of the Jaufre legend, and celebrates him in verse (see Bianchi). In his essay he pays homage to another Italian, Leopardi, whose *Consalvo* contains significant parallels with the Jaufre legend.

In the twentieth century the castle of Blaye and the distant love appear in the *Cantos* of Ezra Pound (Canto 65, p. 371), where Jaufre is briefly mentioned. Most recently, Jaufre appears in Alfred Döblin's novel, *Hamlet*.

Editorial Policy for This Text and Translation

This edition differs from Stimming's in not being in principle simply a conglomerate of the best readings, with no base manuscript. It differs from Jeanroy's edition in not using C as the base for every poem except No. 3, in containing graphies more faithful to the base manuscript than are Jeanroy's, and in the choice of some readings. We also differ from Monaci's choice of base manuscripts for Nos. 1, 3, 5, and 6. We differ from Pickens in not treating every graphic version found in the manuscripts as a separate poetic version. We consider that there is not more than one basic version for any of the six songs (with the possible exception of No. 5); the manuscripts contain more or less corrupt versions, and some manuscripts contain stanzas which we follow tradition in judging to be apocryphal: most of the interpolated stanzas, from a stylistic point of view, are clearly not Jaufre's. Essentially, we choose a base manuscript for graphic uniformity but are not committed solely to that manuscript for substantive readings.

We assume, except in one case, that the corpus of Jaufre's poems is uncontroversial, and we follow tradition in attributing them to him. Jaufre's style is quite recognizable, and the pervasive theme of the distant love further helps to consolidate the corpus. We take the biographer's judgment of *paubres motz* (poor words) to be significant and characteristic of Jaufre's poetry: the style is simple, and wholly lacks exotic or esoteric words. It is for this reason, as well as for its meter, that we reject *Qui no sap esser chantaire*. This song is much more in the vein of later troubadours, such as Raimbaut of Orange, who would be expected to use such complex words as *laire*, *bauza*, *sauza*, *acatat*, an image such as *bat fer freg* (beats cold iron), and to mention *fals amador* (false lovers), who do not appear as a major theme of Jaufre. Scholars have included this song in the corpus mainly, no doubt, because of its mention of dreaming of the lady (25–27), and of going overseas to see her (28–30). But these commonplaces seem an insufficient basis for ascribing the poem to Jaufre, and it is much more likely that an early scribe, possibly Bernart Amoros, assumed that it was by Jaufre for the same reasons. It may be a partial pastiche of Jaufre, but it is doubtful that Jaufre wrote it.

The choice of base manuscripts is controversial and, according to our view of the tradition, to some degree arbitrary. If any principle is involved, it is that we choose the manuscript which has the greatest number of best readings as well as the best grammar and syntax so far as can be judged. In the case of near-identical versions, such as AB or IK, we use the manuscript which either has the fewer anomalous readings or has the greater sanction of tradition. For example, most often A and B are practically identical, but A has a considerably larger collection of poems and has most consistently been used by editors. Pickens's edition, which prints, annotates, and translates every version (in his sense), is most useful for establishing the best manuscript for each song.

For 1 and 2 (Pickens's 3 and 4; he follows the order of Jeanroy, who followed Stimming) the choice is straightforward: we use C as a base, and supplement with e^3 where C is lacking. The versions of C and e^3 are extremely close. For 3 (Pickens's 6) the version of Ee^3 is clearly the least corrupt. C contains interpolated stanzas, lacks most of stanza 5, and makes an obvious jumble of the middle stanzas. Me^g does the same, and is cut short as well. R lacks the interpolated stanzas but mixes up stanzas 2 and 5 and is generally less careful in

Introduction

its language. The second best version is perhaps a, though it is quite syntactically corrupt and also suffers from interpolation. A and B contain the best version of 4 (Pickens's 2); every other manuscript suffers from interpolation although there is an element of the arbitrary here since there is, in the authentic stanzas, very little deviation in substantive readings, and CMe[b] give, except for the apocryphal stanzas, the same basic text.

For 5 (Pickens's 1) the tradition divides into two forms, one (ABDIKMN²S[g]e[g]) containing the interpolated stanzas "A" and "B," the other (CER) containing stanzas 2 and 3. Here we follow Jeanroy in choosing C as the base (R lacks stanza 6; E is slightly inferior in its readings). A and B are the only manuscripts which contain all eight stanzas of 6 (Pickens's 5). All the other manuscripts except C and R also have conglomerated some of the individual stanzas. This song, however, is another which has comparatively few substantive variants despite the multifariousness of the manuscript representation. It is primarily the stanza order which is controversial. We have chosen C's order for its greater poetic logic, which we interpret as follows. The second stanza introduces the notion of pilgrimage for the first time: the poet's desire to be captured by the Saracens (stanza 5) seems arbitrary without this introduction. Similarly, the mention of *pas* (or *portz*) *e camis* in stanza 4, since it is clearly in a context of pilgrimage, also seems arbitrary without the previous introduction. Moreover, the beginning of stanza 4 tends to presuppose the decision to depart which is provided in stanza 3. There the poet refers to the "distant lodging" which he will seek; and the "distant lodging" is a natural next step once the idea of pilgrimage has been introduced, as in stanza 2. Thus, the hopeful pilgrim's progression is best represented by C's order: the idea of pilgrimage (2), the thought of being sheltered once there (3), the departure of the pilgrim once he has arrived at his destination (4). Stanza 5 seems a natural culmination of the series, where the poet affirms that he is ready to be captured by the Saracens. From this to the invocation to God seems a likely progression; in any event, stanza 6 does not have specifically to do with pilgrimage and so should at least come before or after the series of stanzas 2345. Stanza 7 goes with the envoi, and comes last in all manuscripts which contain it but which lack the envoi.

The order of the poems is also one of the controversial topics of Jaufre studies. Stimming's order conforms to his idea of Jaufre's poetico-biographical development. Jeanroy follows Stimming, and Pickens Jeanroy, for convenience of reference. All editors place Nos. 1 and 2 somewhere in the middle of the corpus, and 1 always precedes 2. We have followed previous editors in placing 1 before 2, but we are the first to place 1 and 2 at the beginning of the corpus. We take these poems to be early efforts of Jaufre. They seem the least spiritual of all the poems, and nowhere make reference to external persons or events. In these two poems the theme of *amor de lonh*, while clearly incipient, is still undeveloped.

We follow the scholars who see references to the crusade in songs 4 and 5. It is likely that No. 4 is sent to Hugh of Lusignan in connection with the latter's departure for the Holy Land; this would have been an excellent reason for mentioning him, especially if Jaufre were himself planning to depart later. We take No. 5 to be written after 4 because of the lines *Amors, alegres part de vos / per so quar vau mo mielhs queren*. This seems to be a reference to the crusade and is followed by a concluding stanza exhorting the worthy to depart for Bethlehem. It is quite possible that the *Bon Guiren* in line 33 is William VI Taillefer, thanks to whom Jaufre was able to go on crusade. The reference is not certain, however. In any event, the lines of Poem 5 quoted above suggest that Jaufre was closer to departure than in Poem 4.

Poem 3 refers to Lord Bertrand, taken by scholars to be the bastard son of Alphonse-Jourdain, "in Quercy," and to Alphonse-Jourdain himself "in Toulouse." If Bertrand was in Quercy and Alphonse-Jourdain in Toulouse at the time, then this song must pre-date August of 1147, when Alphonse-Jourdain set sail for Acre. Since there is not yet any mention of the crusade, it seems likely that No. 3 pre-dates the songs which do mention the crusade, and so should be placed before them. This leaves No. 6, which we take to be a culmination of Jaufre's literary achievement though there is no real basis for dating it.

Following modern convention, i and j, u and v have been distinguished where only i and u appear in the manuscripts.

Select Bibliography

I. Major Editions and Transcriptions of Manuscripts

Battaglia, Salvatore. *Jaufre Rudel e Bernardo di Ventadorn: Liriche*. Speculum: Raccolta di testi medievali e moderni, 3. Naples, 1949. Order of poems follows Casella.

Bendazzi, Gianalberto. "Canzoni di Jaufre Rudel." *Lettore di Provincia: Testi, ricerche, critica*, 25–26 (1976), 62–72. Jeanroy's text; order of poems 632145.

Bertoni, Giulio. *Il Canzoniere provenzale di Bernart Amoros. Complemento Campori*. Fribourg: Gschwend, 1911, pp. 337–39. Text of 5, 6. (MS. a)

Brakelmann, Julius. "Die altfranzösische Liederhandschrift Nr. 389 der Stadtbibliothek zu Bern." *Archiv für das Studium der Neueren Sprachen und Literaturen*, 42 (1868), 357–58. Text of 4. (MS. h)

Casella, Mario. *Jaufre Rudel: Liriche*. Florence: Fussi, 1946. Order of poems 346125; mostly follows Jeanroy for the text; interpretative and musical notes.

Gauchat, L. "Les poésies provençales conservées par des chansonniers français." *Romania*, 22 (1893), 393. Text of 6. (MS. W)

Grützmacher, G. "Die provenzalische Liederhandschrift der Laurenziana Bibliothek in Florenz." *Archiv für das Studium der Neueren Sprachen und Literaturen*, 35 (1864), 450–51. Text of 4. (MS. U)

Jeanroy, Alfred. *Les Chansons de Jaufre Rudel*. CFMA, 15. Paris: Champion, 1915; 2nd ed. 1924. Order of poems follows Stimming.

Lecoy, Felix. *Jean Renart: Le Roman de la Rose ou de Guillaume de Dôle*. CFMA, 91. Paris: Champion, 1962, p. 41, lines 1301–07. (MS. ϵ)

Mahn, Carl A.F. *Gedichte der Troubadours in provenzalischer Sprache*. 4 vols. Berlin, 1856; rpt. Geneva: Slatkine; I, 53, 87, 90. Text of 4, 5, 6. (MS. B)

Meyer, Paul, and Gaston Raynaud. *Le Chansonnier français de Saint-Germain des Prés.* SATF, 32. Paris, 1892. Fol. 81v; facsimile of 6, with music. (MS. X)

Monaci, Ernesto. *Poesia e vita di Jaufre Rudel.* Testi romanzi per uso delle scuole, fasc. 5. Rome, 1903. Order of poems 36412, *Qui no sap*, 5, *vida*.

Mussafia, Adolfo. "Del codice Estense di rime provenzali." *Sitzungsberichte der königlichen Akademie der Wissenschaften zu Wein*, Phil.-Hist. Klasse, 55 (1867), 434–35. Text of 4. (MS. D)

Pakscher, A., and Cesare De Lollis. "Il canzoniere provenzale A (Cod. Vaticano 5232)." *Studj di Filologia Romanza*, 3 (1891), 393–96; "Il canzoniere provenzale B," 700–1. Text of *vida*, 4, 5, 6. (MSS. A, B)

Pellegrini, Silvio. "Un frammento inedito di canzoniere provenzale." *Anuario de Estudios Medievales* (Barcelona), 4 (1967), 390; also in *Studi Mediolatini e Volgari*, 15–16 (1968), 96–97. Text of 6. (MS. M^a)

Pickens, Rupert T. *The Songs of Jaufre Rudel.* Studies and Texts, 41. Toronto: Pontifical Institute of Medieval Studies, 1978. Order of poems follows Jeanroy; prints every manuscript version.

Pillet, Alfred. "Die altprovenzalische Liederhandschrift N^2 (Cod. Phillipps 1910 der königlichen Bibliothek zu Berlin), III." *Archiv für das Studium der Neueren Sprachen und Literaturen*, 102 (1899), 192–93. Text of *vida* and 5. (MS. N^2)

Richter, Reinhilt. *Die Troubadourzitate im Breviari d'Amor: kritische Ausgabe der provenzalischen Überlieferung.* Modena: S.T.E.M.-Mucchi, 1976, p. 303. Quotes stanza 2 of No. 3. (MS. α)

Ricketts, Peter T. *Le Breviari d'Amor de Matfre Ermengau*, tome V (27252T–34597). Leiden: Brill, 1976. Quotes stanza 2 of No. 3 (29417–22). (MS. α)

Shepard, William P. *The Oxford Provençal Chansonnier.* Elliott Monographs in the Romance Languages and Literatures, 21. Princeton, 1927; pp. 169–70. Text of 4, 6. (MS. S)

Stimming, Albert. *Der Troubadour Jaufre Rudel, sein Leben und seine Werke.* Berlin, 1873. Order of poems 541263.

II. English Translations and Major Anthologies

Appel, Carl. *Provenzalische Chrestomathie.* 6th ed. Leipzig, 1930; rpt. Olms; pp. 54–55. Text of 6.

Audiau, Jean, and René Lavaud. *Nouvelle Anthologie des troubadours.* Paris: 1928; pp. 23–28. Text and trans. of 4, 6.

Bartsch, Karl. *Chrestomathie provençale.* 6th ed. rev. E. Koschwitz. Marburg, 1904; rpt. AMS; cols. 59–60. Text of 4.

Bec, Pierre. *Nouvelle Anthologie de la lyrique occitane du moyen âge.* 2nd ed. Avignon: Aubanel, 1972; pp. 177–85. Text of *vida*, text and trans. of 4, 6.

Blackburn, Paul. *Proensa: An Anthology of Troubadour Poetry.* Berkeley: California, 1978; pp. 67–71. Trans. of 4, 6.

Bonner, Anthony. *Songs of the Troubadours.* New York: Schocken, 1972; pp. 61–67. Trans. of 2, 4, 6.

Costello, Louisa S. *Specimens of the Early Poetry of France from the Time of the Troubadours and Trouvères to the Reign of Henri Quatre.* London, 1835; pp. 14–15. Trans. of stanzas 1–3 of 1.

Flores, Angel. *An Anthology of Medieval Lyrics.* New York: Modern Library, 1962; pp. 25–29. Trans. of 3 (Harvey Birenbaum), 4 (Maurice Valency), 6 (William M. Davis).

———. *Medieval Age.* New York: Dell, 1963; pp. 176–78. Trans. of 6 (Muriel Kittel).

Goldin, Frederick. *Lyrics of the Troubadours and Trouvères.* New York: Doubleday, 1973; rpt. Smith; pp. 100–107. Text and trans. of 4, 6.

Hamlin, Frank R., Peter T. Ricketts, and John Hathaway. *Introduction à l'étude de l'ancien provençal.* Geneva: Droz; pp. 87–94. Text of *vida*, 1, 6.

Hill, Raymond T., and Thomas G. Bergin. *Anthology of the Provençal Troubadours.* New Haven: Yale, 1941. 2nd ed. 2 vols. 1973; I, 31–36. Text of 1, 3, 4, 6.

Lommatzsch, Erhard. *Leben und Lieder der provenzalischen Troubadours.* 2 vols. Berlin: Akademie, 1957; I, 6–8, 152–53. Text and music of 4, 6.

Mahn, Carl A.F. *Die Werke der Troubadours in provenzalischer Sprache.* 4 vols. Berlin, 1846–53; I, 61–66. Prints all of Raynouard's texts.

Moffett, Martha L. *Love Poems of the Troubadours.* New York and Cleveland: World, 1971; pp. 82–87. Trans. of 1 (Louisa S. Costello), 6 (from 19th cent. sources).

Nelli, René, and René Lavaud. *Les Troubadours.* 2 vols. Bruges: Desclée de Brouwer, 1960, 1966; II, 48–54. Text and trans. of 4, 6.

Press, Alan R. *Anthology of Troubadour Lyric Poetry*. Austin: Texas, 1971; pp. 30–39. Text and trans. of 3, 4, 5, 6.

Purcell, Sally. *Provençal Poems*. Oxford: Carcanet, 1969; pp. 34–35. Trans. of 6.

Raynouard, François J.M. *Choix des poésies originales des troubadours*. 6 vols. Paris, 1816–21; rpt. Osnabruck; III, 94–103. Text of 1, 2, 3, 4, 6; text of *vida* in V, 165.

Riquer, Martín de. *Los Trovadores*. 3 vols. Barcelona: Editorial Planeta, 1975; I, 15–69. Text and trans. of *vida*, 1, 3, 4, 5, 6.

Rochegude, Henri-Pascal de. *Le Parnasse occitanien*. Toulouse, 1817; pp. 19–22. Text of *vida*; text and trans. of 1.

Roncaglia, Aurelio. *Venticinque poesie dei primi trovatori*. Testi e manuali, 28. Modena: S.T.E.M., 1949; pp. 47–56. Text of *vida* 1, 3, 4, 6.

Smythe, Barbara. *Trobador Poets: Selections from the Poems of Eight Trobadors*. London, 1929; rpt. Cooper Square; pp. 11–24. Trans. of 3, 4, 5, 6.

Trask, Willard R. *Medieval Lyrics of Europe*. New York and Cleveland: New American Library, 1969; pp. 25–26. Trans. of 6.

Wilhelm, James J. *Medieval Song: An Anthology of Hymns and Lyrics*. New York: Dutton, 1971; pp. 130–34. Trans. of 3, 6.

III. Critical Writings and Related Works

Allegretto, Manuela. *Il luogo dell'amore. Studio su Jaufre Rudel*. Biblioteca dell'Archivum Romanicum, serie 1, *146*. Florence: Olschki, 1979. Literary analysis, with emphasis on syntactical features.

Andrae, A. "Weiterleben und Verbreitung einiger alten Stoffe." *Romanische Forschungen*, 27 (1910), 351. Mentions the authors who deal with the theme of *amor de loing*.

Andresen, Hugo. *Zu Jaufre Rudel*. Halle, 1917. Prefers *val* to *vau* at 4.11.

Appel, Carl. "Wierderum zu Jaufre Rudel." *Archiv für das Studium der Neueren Sprachen und Literaturen*, 107 (1901), 338–49. Argues for the Virgin Mary as the *amor de loing*.

Barbieri, Giovanni M. *Dell'origine della poesia rimata*. Ed. G. Tiraboschi. Modena, 1790; pp. 71–72. Recounts the legend and quotes from Jaufre's poems.

Select Bibliography

Barrington, Michael. *Blaye, Roland, Rudel, and the Lady of Tripoli.* Salisbury: Bennett, 1953. Rambling treatment of the legend and the poems, in the context of the Crusade, and of Blaye.

Bastero, Antonio. *La crusca provenzale.* Rome, 1724.

Battaglia, Salvatore. *La coscienza letteraria del Medioevo.* Naples: Liguori, 1965, pp. 241–62. Survey of the poetic and spiritual aspects of Jaufre's oeuvre.

Bertoni, Giulio. "Due poesie di Jaufre Rudel." *Zeitschrift für Romanische Philologie,* 35 (1911), 533–42. Edits a's version of 3, and *Qui no sap esser chantaire.*

———. Review of Jeanroy (1915). *Annales du Midi,* 27 (1915), 217–22. For details see Textual Notes.

Bianchi, Lorenzo. "Commento a tre liriche carducciane." *Convivium,* 25 (1957), 564–70. Critical ed. and discussion of Carducci's poem.

Blum, P. "Der Troubadour Jaufre Rudel und sein Fortleben in der Literatur." *Jahresbericht der 2. Königlichen Staatsrealschule in Brünn,* 1912. Surveys the legend, as well as the works of Uhland, Heine, Carducci and Rostand.

Bond, Gerald A. *The Poetry of Count William VII of Poitiers, IX Duke of Aquitaine.* New York: Garland, 1982.

Bouillon, E. Review of Crescini (1890). *Romania,* 19 (1890), 500–501. Approves.

Boussard, Jacques, ed. *Historia pontificum et comitum engolismensium.* Paris: D'Argences, 1957.

Braet, Herman. Review of Pickens (1978). *Romanische Forschungen,* 92 (1980), 448–49. Brief, favorable review.

Browning, Robert. *Poetry and Prose.* Oxford: Clarendon, 1941.

Burger, André. "*Lanquand li jorn son lonc en mai*: une chanson d'amour et de croisade." *Mélanges René Crozet.* 2 vols. Poitiers, 1966; II, 777–80. Comments on Lejeune's edition.

Carducci, Giosue. "Jaufre Rudel, poesia antica e moderna." *Edizione Nazionale delle Opere;* VII, 205–38; (also Bologna, 1888). Discusses Leopardi's *Consalvo;* traces history of the legend.

Casella, Mario. "Poesia e storia: II, Jaufre Rudel." *Archivio Storico Italiano,* 96 (1938, vol. 2), 153–99. Criticizes Jeanroy and Paris for insensitive assessment of Jaufre; argues that the *amor de loing* has a purely spiritual existence, and is a reflection of Jaufre himself.

Cherchi, Paolo. "Notula sull'amore lontano di Jaufre Rudel." *Cultura Neolatina*, 32 (1972), 185–87. Adduces parallel in St. Augustine for falling in love by hearsay.

Cluzel, Irenée M. "Jaufre Rudel et l'*amor de lonh*." *Romania*, 78 (1957), 86–97. Argues that Jaufre, having met "a lady" on Crusade, took a second trip to the Holy Land; proposes new order of poems.

———. Review of Lejeune (1959). *Cahiers de Civilisation Médiévale*, 3 (1960), 363–65. Brief survey of the legend and its scholarship, followed by a description of Lejeune's article.

Cocito, Luciana. *Jaufre Rudel e Hugon Brun*. Genoa: Typis, 1953.

———. *Pagine di letteratura romanza*. Genoa: Bozzi, 1967; pp. 197–205. Edition of 4.

———. "Una nota rudelliana." *Convivium*, 37 (1969), 470–75. Argues that the last stanza of 4 was added by a later jongleur and refers to events which took place at the beginning of the 13th century.

Condren, Edward I. "The Troubadour and his Labor of Love." *Mediaeval Studies*, 34 (1972), 174–95. Suggests that the poems are about desire in general rather than about a real-life lady.

Cravayat, Paul. "Les Origines du troubadour Jaufre Rudel." *Romania*, 71 (1950), 166–79. Gives the facts about Jaufre's life.

Crescimbeni, Giovanni M. *L'istoria della volgar poesia*. Rome, 1698.

Crescini, Vincenzo. "Appunti su Jaufre Rudel." *Atti e Memorie della Regia Accademia di Scienze, Lettere ed Arti in Padova*, Nuova Serie, 6. Padova, 1890; 177–90. Argues against Suchier; see Textual Notes.

———. "Jaufre Rudel." *Per gli studi romanzi*. Padova, 1892; pp. 1–18.

Crist, Larry S. "*Dieu ou ma dame*: The Polysemic Object of Love in Jaufre Rudel's *Lanquan li jorn*." *Marche Romane*, 29 (1979), 61–75. Analyzes 6 structurally.

De Lollis, Cesare. Review of Appel (1901). *Studj di Filologia Romanza*, 9 (1903), 476–77. Noncommittal description.

Del Monte, Alberto. "*En durmen sobre chevau*." *Filologia Romanza*, 2 (1955), 140–47. On reality and dream visions in Jaufre.

Diament, Henri. "De la possibilité d'une structure sémantico-syntaxique hébraique dans la langue des troubadours provençaux." *Romance Notes*, 20 (1979–80), 125–34. On the phrase *jauzitz jauzen* [Ed. Jeanroy].

Diez, Friedrich C. *Leben und Werke der Troubadours.* Leipzig, 1829. 2nd ed., 1882; rpt. Olms, pp. 46–53. Identifies the Countess of Tripoli with Melisende, and the *coms en Tolza* with Raymond V.

Döblin, Alfred. *Hamlet; oder, Die lange Nacht nimmt ein Ende.* Berlin: Rütten & Loening, 1956.

Dragonetti, Roger. "*Aizi* et *aizimen* chez les plus anciens troubadours." *Mélanges Maurice Delbouille.* Gembloux, 1964; II, 127–53. Discusses *aizi* in Jaufre.

Dresden, S. *Het probleem der literaire werkelijkheid "La princesse lointaine."* Leidse Voordrachten, *15*. Leiden, 1954.

Egan, Margarita. Review of Pickens (1978). *Speculum*, 55 (1980), 172–73. Favorable.

FEW: See Wartburg

Frank, Grace. "The Distant Love of Jaufre Rudel." *Modern Language Notes*, 57 (1942), 528–34. Argues that the *amor de loing* means love of the Holy Land, personified as love of a faraway mistress.

———. "Jaufre Rudel, Casella and Spitzer." *Modern Language Notes*, 59 (1944), 526–31. Pleads for a plurality of approaches to medieval texts, unrestricted to Spitzer's and Casella's aesthetic and metaphysical approaches.

Gegou, Fabienne. "Jean Renart et la lyrique occitane." *Mélanges Pierre le Gentil.* Paris, 1973; 319–23. Discusses 1 as it appears in *Guillaume de Dôle*.

———. "Stendhal et l'amour en 'Provence' au Moyen Age." *Cultura Neolatina*, 38 (1978), 95–104. *Amor de loing* illustrates Stendhal's theories on crystallization.

Heine, Heinrich. *Werke.* Berlin-Paris: Akademie Verlag-Editions du C.N.R.S., 1979.

Heisig, Karl. "Zur Biographie von Jaufre Rudel." *Die Neueren Sprachen*, N.F., 8 (1959), 367–69. Adduces Arabic, Greek, etc., parallels for the "distant princess" theme but nowhere mentions Zade.

Hoepffner, Ernest. "Pour l'étude de Jaufre Rudel." *Romania*, 63 (1937), 93–102. Remarks on 3; refines Ortiz' stylistic comparison with William IX.

———. *Les Troubadours dans leurs vies et dans leurs oeuvres*. Paris: Colin, 1955. Summary presentation.

Jeanroy, Alfred. "Sur quelques textes provençaux récemment publiés." *Romania*, 41 (1912), 107–108. Comments on Bertoni's new texts of 3 and *Qui no sap esser chantaire*.

———. *La Poésie lyrique des troubadours*. 2 vols. Toulouse and Paris, 1934; rpt. Slatkine, II, 17–20. Believes the biography completely fictional; calls poems beginning of hermetic poetry.

Julien-Laferrière, P. "Les familles des sires de Blaye aux environs de 1300." *Généalogies du Sud-Ouest*, 8 (1979), 10–14.

Köhler, Erich. "*Amor de lonh*, oder: Der 'Prinz' ohne Burg." *Orbis Medievalis: Mélanges R.R. Bezzola*. Bern, 1978; pp. 219–34. Explains the *amor de loing* in terms of the aspirations of the petty knighthood toward integration with the established aristocracy.

Lacombe, Henri. "Du troubadour Rigaut de Barbezieux au troubadour Jaufre Rudel." *Société Archéologique et Historique de la Charente, Angoulême. Mémoires*. Année 1961–62; pp. 205–13. Historical summary.

Lavisse, Ernest. *Histoire de France*. 9 vols. Paris: Hachette, 1911.

Lefay-Toury, Marie-Noël. "La conscience littéraire chez Jaufre Rudel." *Voyage, Quête, Pélerinage dans la Littérature et la Civilisation Médiévales. Senefiance*, 2 (1976), 413–30. Argues against any attempt to introduce chronological order into the poems; emphasizes Jaufre's self-conscious literary attitude.

Lefèvre, Yves. "Jaufre Rudel, professeur de morale." *Annales du Midi*, 78 (1966), 415–22. Emphasizes Jaufre's moralizing lines.

———. "L'*Amors de terra lonhdana* dans les chansons de Jaufre Rudel." *Mélanges Rita Lejeune*. 2 vols. Gembloux: Duculot, 1969; I, 185–96. Argues for the Holy Land as the key to the *amor de loing*.

———. "Jaufre Rudel et son 'amour de loin.'" *Mélanges Pierre le Gentil*. Paris, 1973; 461–77. Sees the *amor de loing* as the love of the Heavenly Jerusalem; sees only 1 as profane.

Lejeune, Rita. "La chanson de l''amour de loin' de Jaufre Rudel." *Mélanges Angelo Monteverdi*. 2 vols. Modena: S.T.E.M., 1959; I, 403–42. Complete edition based on MS. B; see Textual Notes.

Leopardi, Giacomo. *Opere*. 2 vols. Milan: Ricciardi, 1956–66.

Levy. Emil. *Petit Dictionnaire provençal-français*. 5th ed. Heidelberg: Winter, 1973. (PD)

———. *Provenzalisches Supplement-Wörterbuch*. 8 vols. Leipzig: Reisland, 1894–1924; rpt. Olms. (SW)

———. Review of Stimming. *Literaturblatt für Germanische und Romanische Philologie*, 8 (1887), cols. 80–81. Makes a few minor suggestions about the text.

Lewent, Kurt. "Old Provençal *desmentir sos pairis*." *Modern Language Notes*, 72 (1957), 189–93. Traces Jaufre's influence on a passage of Guilhem Ademar.

———. "On a Passage of Jaufre Rudel." *Modern Language Notes*, 76 (1961), 525–32. Traces Jaufre's influence on a passage of Guilhem de St. Didier.

Lods, Jeanne. Review of Frank (1942) and Spitzer (1944). *Romania*, 71 (1950), 117–18. Summarizes both sides of the debate; sees advantages in each.

Majorano, Matteo. "Lingua e ideologia nel canzoniere di Jaufres Rudels." *Instituto Universitario Orientale, Napoli: Annali, Sezione Romanza*, 16 (1974), 159–201. Comments on each poem from the point of view of the relationship between lyric and social reality and ideology.

Meneghetti, Maria Luisa. "Una vita pericolosa. La 'mediazione' biografica e l'interpretazione della poesia di Jaufre Rudel." *Cultura Neolatina*, 40 (1980), 145–63. Argues against reconstructing the life from the poems; emphasizes the literary critical activity of the biographer.

Meyer, Paul. *Les derniers Troubadours de la Provence d'après le chansonnier donné à la Bibliothèque impériale par M. Ch. Giraud*. Paris, 1871, [Extracted from *Bibliothèque de l'Ecole des Chartes*, 30 (1869), 245–97, 461–534, 649–87; 31 (1870), 412–62].

Monaci, Ernesto. "Ancora di Jaufre Rudel." *Rendiconti della Reale Accademia dei Lincei*, Classe di Scienze Morali, Storiche, e Filologiche. Serie quinta, 2 (1893), 927–43. See Textual Notes.

Moore, Olin H. "Jaufre Rudel and the Lady of Dreams." *Publications of the Modern Language Association*, 29 (1914), 517–36. Agrees with Paris that Jaufre's use of the theme of *amor de loing* is strictly conventional.

Morichi, Tiziana. "La deissi spaziale in Jaufre Rudel e in Bernardo di Ventadorn." *Atti dell'Istituto Veneto di Scienze, Lettere ed Arti*, 135

(1976–77), 565–78. Examines pronominal and adverbial deictic elements and their significance with respect to space and time in Jaufre.

Müller, Ulrich. "Lügende Dichter? (Ovid, Jaufre Rudel, Oswald von Wolkenstein)." *Mélanges Fritz Martini*. Stuttgart, 1969, 32–50. Author of Jaufre's *vida* mistook poetic fiction in the poems for biography.

Nelli, René. *L'Erotique des troubadours*. Toulouse: Privat, 1963; 2 vols. rpt. 10/18. Jaufre in the context of courtly love ca. 1150.

Nykl, Alois R. Review of Spitzer (1944). *Speculum*, 20 (1945), 252–58. Says little about Spitzer; gives his own overview of Jaufre.

Ortiz, Ramiro. "Bons sons ab paubres motz." *Biblioteca degli Studiosi*. Naples, 1909. (Rpt. in author's *Varia Romanica*, Firenze, 1932, pp. 84–108). Argues that *paubres motz* refers to Jaufre's subject matter, not his style.

———. "Intorno a Jaufre Rudel." *Zeitschrift für Romanische Philologie*, 35 (1911), 543–54. (Rpt. in author's *Varia Romanica*, pp. 68–83). Finds similarities between Jaufre and William IX; follows Monaci and Savj-Lopez in taking the *amor de loing* to be terrestrial.

———. "Da Jaufre Rudel ai trovatori armeni." *Zeitschrift für Romanische Philologie*, 45 (1925), 714–25. (Rpt. in author's *Varia Romanica*, pp. 109–23). Brusque change of tone from profane to sacred at the song's end is found in Jaufre and in some Armenian poets; Armenian poets also "sign" their poems.

———. "Jaufre Rudel e i giullari." *Cultura Neolatina*, 3 (1943), 59–70. Discusses references to Peironet and Fillol; see Textual Notes.

Paden, William D., Jr. "Utrum Copularentur: Of Cors." *L'Esprit Créateur*, 19 (1979), 70–83. Ambiguity as the structural principle of Jaufre's art.

Paris, Gaston. "Jaufre Rudel." *Revue Historique*, 53 (1893), 225–60. (Rpt. in *Mélanges de littérature française du moyen âge*, pp. 498–538). Treats the biography as a medieval romance based on the poems; the *razos* are "romanesque inventions."

Payen, Jean Ch. "Peregris. De l'*amor de lonh* au congé courtois." *Cahiers de Civilisation Médiévale*, 17 (1974), 247–55. Suggests that songs of a distant love are to be seen in a context of songs of pilgrimage, and hence of crusade songs.

Peirone, Luigi. "Il sogno d'amore di Jaufre Rudel." *Giornale Italiano di Filologia*, 9 (1956), 64–70. Argues that the women sung by troubadours are "poetic dreams"; links between practical life and lyrical life are tenuous; sides with Spitzer.

———. "Note Dantesche: 1. Echi di Jaufre Rudel nella *Divina Commedia.*" *Giornale Italiano di Filologia,* 19 (1966), 16–18. Seeks to link 3.13–15 to Purg. 8.1–6.

Pellegrini, Silvio. "Jaufre Rudel e la critica." *Mélanges Mario Fubini.* 2 vols. Padua, 1970; I, 234–39. Argues against discounting sensual passages as necessarily non-spiritual; advances the possibility of reading 6 on two planes, amorous and political; argues against ordering the poems around a supposed life of the poet.

———. "Appunti (forse provisori) su Jaufre Rudel." *Studi Mediolatini e Volgari,* 18 (1970), 77–80. Argues against attempting to reduce Jaufre's corpus to a single, unified interpretation.

Pickens, Rupert T. "Jaufre Rudel et la poétique de la mouvance." *Cahiers de Civilisation Médiévale,* 20 (1977), 323–37. Argues that the accidents and changes to Jaufre's text over the ages render vain any attempt at restitution of the original versions of the poems: each transmitter recreates the poem; it is the function of "mouvance" to transform the text.

Pirot, François. *Recherches sur les connaissances littéraires des troubadours occitans et catalans des XIIe et XIIIe siècles: Les sirventes-ensenhamens de Guerau de Cabrera, Guiraut de Calanson, et Bertran de Paris.* Memorias de la Real Academia de Buenas Letras de Barcelona, 14. Barcelona, 1972.

Pound, Ezra. *The Cantos.* New York: New Directions, 1972.

Raynouard, François J.M. *Lexique roman.* 6 vols. Paris, 1836–44; rpt. Winter.

Restori, A. "Jaufre Rudel." *Per l'Arte,* 6, No. 7 (1894). Emphasizes the validity of the aesthetic and poetic aspects of the legend.

Richard, Jean. *Le Comté de Tripoli sous la dynastie toulousaine, 1102–1187.* Paris, 1945; rpt. AMS.

Riley, A.W. "Jaufre Rudel in Alfred Döblin's Last Novel *Hamlet.*" *Mosaic* (Winter, 1977), 131–45. Traces source of Döblin's knowledge of the legend to a book by W.C. Meller.

Robertson, Durant W. "*Amors de terra lonhdana.*" *Studies in Philology,* 49 (1952), 566–82. Argues that Jaufre's poems comprise an allegory of current theological themes, centering around the equation of the lady with the Virgin Mary and the *amor de loing* with the love of the Celestial Jerusalem.

Rostand, Edmond. *La Princesse lointaine.* Paris: Imprimerie de l'Illustration, 1929.

Runciman, Steven. *A History of the Crusades.* 3 vols. Cambridge, 1952; rpt. Penguin.

Sabatier, Ernest. *Jaufre Rudel.* Mémoire de l'Académie de Nimes. 7th Series, 4, 1881, 119–40. Attempts to reconstruct the life from the poems.

Sainte-Palaye, La Curne de. *Histoire littéraire des troubadours.* Ed. Millot. 3 vols. Paris, 1774; I, 85–96. Recounts legend; points out fictions and inconsistencies of Nostredame.

Sanna, Antonio. "Jaufre Rudel e l'amore lontano." *Annali della Facoltà di Lettere, Filosofia e Magistero della Università di Cagliari,* 18 (1951), 331–64. Argues against Appel.

Santangelo, Salvatore. "L'amore lontano di Jaufre Rudel." *Siculorum Gymnasium,* N.S. 6 (1953), 1–28. Critical review of all the theories on the nature and identity of the *amor de loing*.

———. "Jaufre Rudel: *Qui no sap esser chantaire.*" *Mélanges Angelo Monteverdi.* 2 vols. Modena, 1959; II, 681–90. (Rpt. in *Studii, rassegne, varietà: pagine sparse,* Padua, 1963). Edits this poem.

———. "Un preteso canto di crociata di Jaufre Rudel." *Siculorum Gymnasium,* 15 (1962), 137–47. Criticizes Lejeune's ed. of 6, and re-edits it.

Satō, Teruo. "Jofurē Rudēru no l'amor de lonh ni tsuite." *Meisei Daigaku Kenkyū Kiyō: Jimbun Gakubu,* 10 (Oct. 26, 1974), 31–45. Translation of Song 6 and presentation of the distant love theme in historical context.

Savj-Lopez, Paolo. "Jaufre Rudel. Questioni vecchie e nuove." *Rendiconti della Reale Accademia dei Lincei.* Classe di Scienze Morali, Storiche e Filologiche, Serie quinta, 11 (1902), 212–25. (Further developed as "Mistica profana" in *Trovatori e poeti: studi di lirica antica,* Palermo, 1906). Argues against Appel and Monaci; edits the newly discovered *Qui no sap esser chantaire.*

Schultz[-Gora], Oskar. Review of Paris (1893). *Archiv für das Studium der Neueren Sprachen und Literaturen,* 92 (1894), 218–33. Describes and agrees with Paris' article.

Seguy, Jean. Review of Suguy. *Annales du Midi,* 69 (1957), 179. Brief description of this Japanese article.

Serper, Arié. "Les Troubadours Jaufre Rudel et Guilhem Ademar." *Revue des Langues Romanes,* 80 (1973), 405–11. Follows Lewent (1957).

Simonelli, Maria. "Due note rudelliane." *Cultura Neolatina,* 25 (1965), 113–27. Suggests influence of Jaufre on *Bele Erembors* and on Arnaut Daniel.

Smith, Nathaniel B. *Figures of Repetition in the Old Provençal Lyric: A Study in the Style of the Troubadours*. North Carolina Studies in the Romance Languages and Literatures, 176. Chapel Hill, 1976.

Spitzer, Leo. *L'Amour lointain de Jaufre Rudel et le sens de la poésie des troubadours*. University of North Carolina Studies in the Romance Languages and Literatures, 5. Chapel Hill, 1944. (Revised in *Romanische Literaturstudien 1936–56*, Tübingen, 1959, pp. 363–417.). Argues against Frank (1942), and for the notion that the *amor de loing* is the nature of love itself, in which lust conflicts with an ideal state.

———. Review of Santangelo (1953). *Romania*, 75 (1954), 396–402. Attacks S.'s thesis, taken from Monaci, that the *amor de loing* is Eleanor of Aquitaine.

———. Review of Zorzi (1955). *Romania*, 77 (1956), 109–12. Approves of Zorzi's interpretation, which he sees as close to his own.

Staaft, E. "Jaufre Rudel. Ett blad ur trubadurdiktningens historia." *Nordisk Tidskrift för Vetenskap, Konst och Industri*, Stockholm (1919), 241–58. General survey of Jaufre's life and poetry, and of Jaufre scholarship.

Stengel, Edmund. Review of Stimming (1873). *Jenaer Literaturzeitung*, 28 (1874), 430. Severe review, largely dwelling on S.'s superficial classification of manuscripts.

Stone, Donald M., Jr. "Rudel's *Belhs m'es l'estius*: A New Reading." *Neuphilologische Mitteilungen*, 67 (1966), 137–44. Argues that 2 is about Jaufre's attaining true love, in the form of fidelity.

Suchier, Hermann. Review of Stimming (1873). *Jahrbuch für Romanische und Englische Literatur*, 13 (1874), 337–39. Approves, with some minor corrections; see Textual Notes.

Sugi, Fujio. "Jaufré Rudel ni tsuite." *Furansu Bungaku Kenkyu* (1955), 1–10. Attempts to demonstrate the fictional nature of the *vida*.

Swinburne, Algernon C. *Poetical Works*. Edd. E. Gosse, T.J. Wise. 20 vols. London: Heinemann, 1925–27.

Tavera, Antoine. "*Lanquan li jorn*: l'inépuisable texte." *Hommage à Pierre Nardin. Annales de la Faculté des Lettres et Sciences Humaines de Nice*, 29 (1977), 67–81. Emphasizes the fact that there are several versions of the poem, and likens the structure of each to the rhythmic and emotional progression of a musical score.

Topsfield, Leslie T. "*Jois, Amors* and *Fin'Amors* in the Poetry of Jaufre Rudel." *Neuphilologische Mitteilungen*, 71 (1970), 277–305. In Jaufre the search for *jois* is more important than the experience of *amors*.

———. "Three Levels of Love in the Poetry of the Early Troubadours, Guilhem IX, Marcabru and Jaufre Rudel." *Mélanges Jean Boutière*. 2 vols. Liège: Soledi, 1971; I, 571–87. The level of physical desire; that of dreamlike imagining in which *jois* is illusory; and that level which is transcendental and from which good results flow.

———. *Troubadours and Love*. Cambridge, Eng., 1975; ch. 2. A reprint, expanded, of the first article above.

Uhland, Ludwig. *Gesammelte Werke*. 6 vols. Stuttgart: Cotta, 1892.

Viglione, Francesco. "La leggenda di Janfre [sic] Rudel nei canti dei poeti italiani e stranieri." *Rivista d'Italia*, 19 (1916), 40–66. Literary survey of poets who deal with the legend and with the theme of the *amor de loing*.

Vincenti, Eleonora. *Bibliografia antica dei trovatori*. Milan-Naples: Ricciardi, 1963.

Walpole, Ronald N. "Jaufre Rudel—Who Can Open the Book?" *Romance Philology*, 13 (1959–60), 429–41. Discusses strengths and weaknesses of Lejeune (1959).

Wartburg, Walther von. *Französisches etymologisches Wörterbuch*. 31 vols. Bonn, et al., 1922–date (*FEW*)

Wilhelm, James J. *Seven Troubadours: The Creators of Modern Verse*. University Park and London: Pennsylvania State, 1970; ch. 3. Argues against Catharist interpretation of Jaufre; adduces parallels between 3 and Medieval Latin riddling poems; emphasizes Jaufre's elusiveness and mystery.

Zade, Lotte. *Der Troubadour Jaufre Rudel und das Motiv der Fernliebe in der Weltliteratur*. Ph.D. Dissertation, Univ. of Greifswald, 1919. Traces Jaufre's themes to Indian, Oriental, Italian, French, English and German literature, and attempts to show that they are universal folk themes.

Zanella, E. *Jaufre Rudel e Consalvo*. Legnago, 1897. Draws parallels between Leopardi's poem and Jaufre.

Zorzi, Diego. "L'*Amor de lonh* di Jaufre Rudel." *Aevum*, 29 (1955), 124–44. Jaufre's *amor* is a reflection of 12th-century ideas, e.g., that of the school of Chartres that the love which flows from God also flows back to Him; thus Jaufre's *amor* is an image of divine creation.

Zumthor, Paul. *Langue et techniques poétiques à l'époque romane*. Paris: Klincksieck, 1963; ch. 4. Analyzes 6 structurally.

Poetry

1. PRO AI DEL CHAN ESSENHADORS

1. Pro ai del chan essenhadors
   entorn mi, et ensenhairitz,
   pratz e vergiers, albres e flors,
   voutas d'auzelhs e lays e critz,
   per lo dous termini suau,   5
   qu'en un petit de joy m'estau,
   don nulhs deportz no·m pot jauzir
   tan cum solatz d'amor valen.

2. Las pimpas sian als pastors,
   et als enfans bordeitz petitz,   10
   e mias sion tals amors
   don ieu sia jauzens jauzitz;
   qu'ieu la sai bona tot aitau
   ves son amic en greu loguau;
   per so·m sen trop soen marrir   15
   quar non ai so qu'al cor n'aten.

3. Luenh es lo castelhs e la tors
   ont elha jay e sos maritz,
   e si per bos cosselhadors
   cosselhan no suy enantitz--   20
   qu'autre cosselhs petit m'en vau,
   aitan n'ay fin talan corau--
   alres no·y a mais del murir,
   s'alqun joy non ai en breumen.

4. Totz los vezis apel senhors   25
   del renh on sos joys fo noyritz,
   e crey que·m sia grans honors,
   quar ieu dels plus envilanitz
   cug que sion cortes leyau;

Love Song

1.

1. I have plenty of song masters
   And song mistresses around me:[1]
   Meadows and orchards, trees and flowers,
   Birds' songs and lays and cries
   For the sweet, gentle season, 5
   And so I settle with a little enjoyment,
   Such that no diversion can gladden me
   As does the company of worthy love.

2. Let the shepherds have their pipes,
   And the children their little games, 10
   And let such loves be mine
   In which I may enjoy and be enjoyed;
   For I know her to be wholly good
   To her lover in a forbidding place:
   Because of this I feel too often afflicted, 15
   For I do not have what my heart hopes for.

3. Far are the castle and the tower
   Where she and her husband lie;
   And if I am not furthered
   By good counselors' advice-- 20
   For any other counsel is worth little to me,
   So true is my heartfelt desire--
   Then there's nothing left but to die,
   If I do not have some enjoyment soon.

4. I call lords all those near 25
   The land where this joy was raised,
   And it must, I think, be a great honor for me,
   For I believe that the most vile
   Are courtly and loyal;

    ves l'amor qu'ins el cor m'enclau   30
    ai bon talant e bon albir,
    e say qu'ilh n'a bon escien.

5. Lai es mos cors, si totz c'aillors
    non a ni sima ni raïtz,
    et en dormen sotz cobertors   35
    es lai ab lieis mos esperitz;
    e s'amor mi revert a mal,
    car ieu l'am tant e liei non cal;
    tost veirai ieu si per sufrir
    n'atendrai mon bon jauzimen.   40

6. Ma voluntat[z] s'en vay lo cors
    la nueit e·l dia esclarzitz
    laïntz per talant de socors,
    mas tart mi ve e tart mi ditz:
    "Amicx," fa·s elha, "gilos brau   45
    an comensat tal batestau
    que sera greus a departir
    tro qu'abduy en siam jauzen."

7. Per so m'en creis plus ma dolors,
    car ieu au lieis en luec[s] aizit[z],   50
    que tan no fauc sospirs e plors
    que sol baizar per escarit[z]
    lo cor no·m tengues san e sau;
    bona es l'amors, e molt per vau,
    e d'aquest mal mi pot guerir   55
    ses gart de metge sapien.

2. mi es e^3 3. a. floritz e^3 10. burdens e^3 12. ieu jauzens sia e^3 13. l'ai bona e^3 15. suy trop soen marritz Ce^3 20. enaizitz e^3 21. p. m'en au e^3 23. non ai mais e^3 26. sest ioi e^3 30. mi clau e^3 33-40. *lacking in* C   41. *the* en *of* s'en *is unclear in* C; e·l cors e^3 43. son cors Ce^3 45. fai ella e^3 46. barestau e^3 49-56. *lacking in* C   53. Que·l cor mi t. e^3

    I have a good affection for and opinion of   30
    The love which I hold in my heart,
    And I know that she is well aware of it.

5. My heart is so much there with her
    That its summit and root are nowhere else,
    And while I sleep under covers   35
    My spirit is there with her;
    And [yet] her love undoes me,
    For I love her so much and it does not matter to her;
    Soon I shall see if by enduring
    I can hope for my enjoyment.   40

6. My will goes quickly
    At night and in daylight
    Into that place, for desire of relief,
    But she comes to me late and says to me:
    "Love," she says, "jealous boors   45
    Have started a dispute
    That will be hard to settle
    To the point where we can enjoy ourselves together."

7. And so my pain grows even greater,
    For I hear her in convenient places;   50
    But I do not sigh and weep so much
    That one single little kiss
    Would not keep me[2] safe and sound;
    Love is good and has great value,
    And can cure me of this ailment   55
    Without the help of a learned doctor.

    [1] Jaufre may here be playing partly on the reflection of the contrast between "masters" and "mistresses" in the masculine and feminine genders of the words in the next two lines.
    [2] Here *lo cors* with following pronoun ·*m* is taken as equivalent to *mos cors*, "me."

2. BELHS M'ES L'ESTIUS E·L TEMPS FLORITZ

1. Belhs m'es l'estius e·l temps floritz
   quan l'auzelh chanton sotz la flor,
   mas ieu tenc l'ivern per gensor
   quar mais de joy mi es cobitz;
   e quant hom ve son jauzimen, 5
   es ben razos e d'avinen
   qu'om sia plus coyndes e guays.

2. Er ai ieu joy e suy jauzitz,
   e restauratz en ma valor,
   e non iray ja mai alhor, 10
   ni non querrai autruy conquistz;
   qu'eras say ben az escien
   que selh es savis qui aten,
   e selh es fols qui trop s'irays.

3. Lonc temps ai estat en dolor, 15
   e de tot mon afar marritz,
   qu'anc no fuy tan fort endurmitz
   que no·m rissides de paor;
   mas aras vey e pes e sen
   que passat ai aquelh turmen, 20
   e non hi vuelh tornar ja mays.

4. Mout mi tenon a gran honor,
   totz selhs cuy ieu n'ey obeditz,
   quar a mon joy suy revertitz,
   e laus en lieys e Dieu e lhor, 25
   qu'er an lur grat e lur prezen,
   e que qu'ieu m'en anes dizen,
   lai mi remanh e lay m'apays.

                    Love Song

                         2.

1. I love summer, the season of flowers,
    When the birds sing beneath the bloom;
    But I consider winter more pleasing,
    For more enjoyment is accorded me;
    And when one sees one's source of joy   5
    It is right and proper
    That one should be more charming and cheerful.

2. Now I have joy and am happy,
    And my honor has been restored,
    And never will I go elsewhere,   10
    And I will not seek others' winnings,
    For now I know indeed
    That whoever waits is wise,
    And whoever frets is a fool.

3. I have long been in distress,   15
    And troubled about my situation
    For never was I so soundly asleep
    That I could not awake from fright;
    But now I see, think, and feel
    That I have come through this ordeal,   20
    And I never want to return to it.

4. All those whom I have obeyed
    Have great respect for me,
    For I am back again with my happiness,
    And praise her and God and them for it;   25
    They[1] now have their thanks and their reward,
    And whatever I may have said about it,
    There I stay and there am satisfied.

5. Mas per so m'en suy escharzitz,
   ja non creyrai lauzenjador;   30
   qu'anc no fuy tan lunhatz d'amor
   qu'er no·n sia sals e gueritz;
   plus savis hom de mi mespren,
   per qu'ieu sai ben az escien
   qu'anc fin'amor home non trays.   35

6. Mielhs mi fora jazer vestitz
   que despollatz sotz cobertor,
   e puesc vos en traire auctor
   la nueyt quant ieu fuy assalhitz;
   totz temps n'aurai mon cor dolen,   40
   quar aissi·s n'aneron rizen,
   qu'enquer en sospir e·n pantays.

7. Mais d'una re soi en error,
   e·n estai mos cors esbaïtz:
   que tot can lo fraire·m desditz   45
   aug autrejar a la seror;
   e nuills hom non a tan de sen
   que puesc'aver cominalmen,
   que ves calque part non biais.

8. El mes d'abril e de pascor,   50
   can l'auzel movon lur dous critz,
   adoncs vueill mos chans si'auzitz:
   et aprendetz lo, chantador!
   e sapchatz tug cominalmen
   qu'ie·m tenc per rics e per manen   55
   car soi descargatz de fol fais.

2. E·ls auzels e^3 11. Ni conquerrai e^3 13. Que sol es
savais e^3 20. passatz sui d'aisel t. e^3 22. m'o t. e^3
23. Tug silh a cui non soi peditz e^3 25. en D. e leis e^3
27. *lacking in* e^3 31. Car non soi tan 1. e^3 39. soi
a. e^3 41. C'aisi·s n' e^3 43-56. *lacking in* C
51. lurs dous e^3

5. But because[2] I have departed from this [torment],
   I will never believe a flatterer;   30
   For I never was so alienated from love
   That now with it I am not healthy and healed;
   A wiser man than I can err,
   Therefore I know well indeed
   That true love never betrayed anyone.   35

6. I should have gone to bed clothed
   Rather than been naked under the covers,
   And I can call for you as testimony
   The night that I was attacked;
   It will always cause me pain,   40
   For they ran away laughing,
   And I still sigh and dream about it.

7. But I[3] myself am troubled
   And bewildered about one thing:
   Everything the brother denies me   45
   I hear the sister grant;
   And yet no one has so much of the sense
   That one can commonly have,
   That one shouldn't lean in some direction.

8. In the month of April, at Eastertime,   50
   When the birds begin their sweet cries,
   Then do I wish my song to be heard:
   So learn it, singers!
   And you should all together know
   That I consider myself rich and well-off   55
   Because I have cast off a senseless burden.

---

[1]*qu'*, which here may possibly be a relative personal pronoun with *lieys e Dieu e lhor* as antecedent, need not be translated.

[2]Also possibly "But for this reason..."

[3]The third person *estai mos cors* is here translated idiomatically.

133

3. NO SAP CHANTAR QUI SO NON DI

1. No sap chantar qui so non di,
   ni vers trobar qui motz no fa,
   ni conois de rima co·s va
   si razo non enten en si;
   mas lo mieus chans comens'aisi: 5
   con plus l'auziretz, mais valra.

2. Nuils hom no·s meravill de mi
   si ieu am so que ja no·m veira,
   que·l cor joi d'autr'amor non a
   mas de cela que anc no vi, 10
   ni per nuill joi aitan no ri;
   e no sai qual bes m'en venra.

3. Colps de joi me fer que m'ausi,
   e ponha d'amor que·m sostra
   la carn, don lo cors magrira; 15
   et anc mais tan greu no·m feri,
   ni per nuill colp tan no langui,
   quar no cove ni no s'esca.

4. Anc tan suau no m'adurmi,
   mos esperitz tost no fos la, 20
   ni tan d'ira non ac de sa,
   mos cors ades no fos aqui;
   mais quan mi resveill al mati,
   totz mos bos sabers mi desva.

5. Ben sai, anc de leis no·m jauzi, 25
   ni ja de mi no·s jauzira,
   ni per son amic no·m tenra,
   ni coven no·m fara de si;

Love Song

3.

1. He cannot sing who makes no tune,
    And he cannot write songs who makes no words,
    And does not know how a rhyme works
    If he does not understand the matter;
    But my own song begins like this: 5
    The more you hear it, the better it becomes.

2. Let no one be amazed at me
    If I love what will never see me,
    For I enjoy none other
    But her whom I have never seen,   10
    And I have never been so happy for any joy,
    And I do not know what good I shall get out of it.

3. A stroke of joy strikes and kills me,
    As does a prick of love which ravages
    My flesh, and makes me grow thin;   15
    And never have I been so stricken
    Or weakened by any blow,
    For it is not right, and does not happen.

4. I have never fallen asleep so soundly
    That my spirit was not soon there,   20
    Nor have I felt so much grief here
    That I was not there right away;
    But when I awake in the morning
    All my pleasure escapes me.

5. I know indeed that I have never had[1] her,   25
    Nor will she ever have me,
    Nor will she consider me her lover,
    Nor will she promise herself to me;

           anc no·m dis ver ni no·m menti,
           ni no sai si ja o fara.   30

6.   Bos es lo vers, anc no·i failli,
     si tot so que·i es ben esta;
     e sel que de mi l'apenra
     gart no·l franha ni no·l pessi;
     e vueill l'auja en Caersi   35
     En Bertrans e·l coms en Tolza.

7.   Bos es lo vers, e faran hi
     calque re don hom chantara.

1. ·l son MRe^{g}e^3 2. ·ls motz MRe^{g}e^3; fai E   3. Ni no sap de MRe^g 5. Pero mos ch. CMe^g 6. v. a a M 8. no veyrai ja CMe^g; q'enquar vist no m'ha R   12. v. a a M 14. Ab p. C   15. lo cor, don la carns C   16. tan fort no m'agri a   17. Ni per autres a   18. e. a a M 19. t. soven Ee^3 20. Que mos CMRe^g 21. de la a 22. Q'ades ab joi no·l fos a   23. Ho quan Ee^3; quan a; mi ressit lo m. R   24. mi trazva a; d. a a M   29. Anc mais nul temps no mi m. Me^g 30. ja mi veira Ee^3; f. a a M 31. Guart si (que res no mi cambi C; non mueva ni camgi Me^g) CMe^g 35. Que si l'auzon CMRe^g; en Lemozi R   36. Lo vescoms ni·l coms en T. C; le coms de T. l'entendra Me^g; l'e. a a M; B. c. lai en T. a   37. Bon er R; lo sos C 38. Quas que don mos chans gensara C; Calsque motz que R.

          She never told me the truth or lied,
          And I do not know if she ever will.   30

6.   The song is good; I have not failed in it,
     And everything that is in it fits;
     And let whoever learns it from me
     Beware of taking it apart and breaking it up;
     And I would like Lord Bertrand in Quercy   35
     And the Count in Toulouse to hear it.[2]

7.   The song is good, and there[3] they will do
     Something that people will sing about.

   [1]*se jauzir de* is here translated by "to have"; cf. *Shorter Oxford English Dictionary, Addenda*, p. 2634.
   [2]The Count is probably Alphonse-Jourdain of Toulouse, and Lord Bertrand Alphonse's bastard son; see Life of the Author.
   [3]"there" may conceivably refer to the Holy Land; see Textual Notes.

4. QAN LO RIUS DE LA FONTANA

1. Qan lo rius de la fontana
    s'esclarzis si cum far sol,
    e par la flors aiglentina,
    e·l rossignoletz el ram
    volv e refraing et aplana   5
    son doutz chantar et afina,
    dreitz es q'ieu lo mieu refraigna.

2. Amors de terra loindana,
    per vos totz lo cors mi dol;
    e non puosc trobar meizina   10
    si non vau al sieu reclam,
    ab atraich d'amor doussana,
    dinz vergier o sotz cortina
    ab desirada compaigna.

3. Pois del tot m'en faill aizina,   15
    no·m meravill s'ieu m'aflam,
    car anc genser Crestiana
    non fo, que Dieus non la vol,
    Juzeva ni Sarrazina;
    et es ben paisutz de manna   20
    qui ren de s'amor gazaigna.

4. De desir mos cors non fina
    vas cella ren q'ieu plus am;
    e cre que volers m'engana
    si cobezeza la·m tol;   25
    que plus es pongens q'espina
    la dolors que ab joi sana,
    don ja non vuoill c'om m'en plaigna.

Love Song

4.

1. When the fountain's flow
   Shines brilliantly as usual,
   And the wild rose appears,
   And the little nightingale on the branch
   Varies, changes, smooths out   5
   And perfects his sweet song,
   It is right that I should rehearse mine.

2. Love from a distant land,
   For you my whole self aches;
   And I can find no remedy   10
   Unless I go at her call,
   With the lure of sweet love,
   In a garden or beneath a curtain
   With a desired companion.

3. Since I get no relief[1] at all,   15
   I am not surprised if I am aflame,
   For there was never a nobler Christian woman,
   A Jewess or a Saracen,
   For God does not wish that there be;
   And whoever gains any of her love   20
   Is well fed with manna.

4. I do not cease desiring
   Her whom I love most,
   And I think my will deceives me
   If lust takes her away from me;   25
   And the pain which is relieved by enjoyment
   Is more piercing than a thorn,
   And I want no one to pity me for it.

5. Senes breu de pargamina
    tramet lo vers que chantam   30
    plan et en lenga romana
    a·N Hugon Brun per Fillol;
    bon m'es car gens Peitavina,
    de Beiriu et de Guianna
    s'esgau per lui, e Bretaigna.   35

1. Pois lo r. SUa   4. Lo r. U   5. veilh' e r. U
6. Son novel ch. s'afina S   9. lo cor CER   11. Tro veng
al vostre r. Me^b; Si no·m (no·i a) val vostre Ea; Si non al
vostre CR   12. Ab maltraig CES   13. (part CE; tras MSS^{g}e^b;
dins RS; sa U) cortina CEMRSS^{g}Ue^b 15. (A, Pos)(totz, quecx)
jorns CEMRSUe^b 16. si·m n'a. R; ieu n'a. DIKS^{g}Ua; ieu a M;
n'ai fam CS   17. Qe tan gensor, en plevina S   18. D. no
la fis ni la·m vol S   20. Per qu'es ben IK; pagutz ASa;
paguatz CU; ben es astrucx qui s'en vana E; er doncx pascutz R
21. Ni re E; Si ja drutz s'amor R   22. De voler MSS^{g}e^b;
Mon c. de valer a   23. V. cel'amor S^g; Cela cui tan voll
et am S   24. E sai MS^{g}e^b; Sai que volontatz m' E; Ben sai
qe voler me mena S   25. E c. ES; Que c. S^g 27. Ma d.
MS^{g}Ue^b; c'al cor mi mena E   29. S'en est breu e^b
30. Enviu mon ch. part Roam a; mon v. E; en chantan ABCEMe^b
31. En plana lenga r. CEMa; plazent l. S^g; en l. latina B
32. Lai a·N Peir'Ug per Sigol a; mon f. S^{g}e^b 33. E sapcha
gens crestiana DIKS^g; Bo·m sap CMe^b; Ben sapcha g. a
34. Que tot Pitieus (Angieus M) DEIKMS^{g}a; hi guazanha E; (et,
o) de Bretaigna ABC   35. Val mais per l. DEIKS^{g}a; E·n val
mais per l. B. E; per lieys CDEIKMS^{g}a; e (en C) Guia(ig)na ABC

5. Without a parchment letter
   I send the song which we sing   30
   Plainly and in Romance tongue
   To Lord Hugh the Swarthy, by Godson;[2]
   And I am glad that the Poitevins,
   The men of Berry, the men of Guyenne,
   And the Bretons rejoice for him.

[1]*aizina* may also mean "opportunity."
[2]The name *Fillol* might also remain untranslated here.

5. QUAN LO ROSSINHOLS EL FOLLOS

1. Quan lo rossinhols el follos
   dona d'amor e·n quier e·n pren,
   e mou son chant jauzent joyos,
   e remira sa par soven,
   e·l riu son clar e·l prat son gen,   5
   pel novel deport que·y renha,
   mi ven al cor grans joys jazer.

2. D'un'amistat suy enveyos--
   quar no sai joya plus valen--
   c'or e dezir, que bona·m fos   10
   si·m fazia d'amor prezen;
   que·l cors a gras, delgat e gen,
   e ses ren que·y descovenha,
   e s'amors bon'ab bon saber.

3. D'aquest'amor suy cossiros   15
   vellan e pueys sompnhan dormen,
   quar lai ay joy meravelos
   per qu'ieu la jau joyos, jauzen;
   mas sa beutatz no·m val nien,
   quar nulhs amicx no m'essenha   20
   cum ieu ja n'aya bon saber.

4. D'aquest'amor suy tan cochos
   que quant ieu vau ves lieys corren,
   vejaire m'es qu'a reüsos
   m'en torn e que lay·s n'an fugen;   25
   e mos cavals y cor tan len...
   a greu cug mais que·y atenha,
   s'amors no la·m fay remaner.

Love Song

5.

1. When the nightingale in the leaves[1]
   Gives, seeks, and takes love,
   And happily begins his song,
   And gazes often at his mate,
   And the streams are clear and the meadows fair,   5
   Because of the new pleasure which prevails,[2]
   A great joy settles in my heart.

2. I am eager for a love affair--
   For I know no more worthy enjoyment--
   Which I pray for and desire, and it would be good   10
   If she made me a gift of love;
   For she has a full body, delicate and fair,
   With nothing that could be unbecoming,
   And her good, pleasurable love.

3. I am preoccupied with this love   15
   Awake and then asleep in dreams,
   For there I have amazing joy,
   Because I enjoy her[3] and am joyously happy;
   But her beauty is worth nothing to me,
   Because no friend will inform[4] me   20
   How I might obtain this pleasure.

4. I am so anxious about this love
   That when I go running towards her
   It seems to me I'm turning
   Backwards and that she's fleeing;   25
   And my horse runs so slowly...
   I do not think I shall ever get there,
   Unless love makes her hold back.

5. Amors, alegres part de vos,
   per so quar vau mo mielhs queren;   30
   e suy en tant aventuros
   qu'enqueras n'ay mon cor jauzen,
   la merce de mon Bon Guiren
   que·m vol e m'apell'e·m denha,
   e m'a tornat en bon esper.   35

6. E qui sai rema deleytos
   e Dieu non siec en Bethleem,
   no sai cum ja mais sia pros,
   ni cum ja venh'a guerimen;
   qu'ieu sai e cre, mon escien,   40
   que selh qui Jhesus ensenha
   segura escola pot tener.

1. rossinhol C   2. d'amar M   7. M. vai g. j. al cor CE
10. Que d'aquesta que C   11. d'amar parven R   12. c. a
gran R   18. jauzens joyos CE   19. beutat C   20. no
la senha R   22. Mas, dura amor, sui a   23. vas luy CR
24. reversos C; qu'en torn aravios E; en r. a   25. e qu'ella
m'an fugen ABDIKN²RS^g 26. vai (ai)tan 1. CMEe^g; sos chiv-
aus cor aitan R   27. G. er cui mais i a. ABDIKN²S^g
28. S'ilha no·s vol aretener (aremaner E) CE; s'ab merce non
vol remaner a   29. alegre·m DEIKN²RS^{g}a   30. Q'ieu sai
q'en vauc a   31. E fui·n al prim tan volontos a
32. Q'enqer n'aurai m. c. ABDIKN²RS^g; en que retrai m. c. E
33. Mas pero per mon CE; Mas pero port mon bon talen a; Bel
G. R   34. Q'enqera m'a. a; vol e·m dezir R   35. M'es
ops (m'esteup E) aparcer mon voler CE; E m'estou partir men
voler a   41. cui Jhesu Crist seinha M   42. S. colpa M

5. Love, I leave you cheerfully,
   For I seek what is best for me;   30
   And I am so fortunate in this
   That I am still rejoicing,
   Thanks to my Good Protector
   Who wants, calls, and approves me,
   And has made me very hopeful.   35

6. And whoever stays here enjoying himself,
   And does not follow God to Bethlehem,
   I do not know how he will ever be worthy,
   Or how he will ever reach salvation;
   For I know and indeed believe   40
   That whoever teaches of Jesus
   Holds a good school.[5]

[1]"Leaves" is given here for the possibly more precise "leafy [woods]," *folhos* being an adjective.
[2]The sense of *y* here is very general, and does not suffer from not being translated.
[3]Also possibly "Because I enjoy it..."
[4]The present *essenha* is translated here with the auxiliary "will," which need not convey a future sense.
[5]Also possibly "whomever Jesus teaches follows a sure path" (Jeanroy).

6. LANQAN LI JORN SON LONC EN MAI

1. Lanqan li jorn son lonc en mai
   m'es bels doutz chans d'auzels de loing,
   e qan me sui partitz de lai,
   remembra·m d'un'amor de loing:
   vau de talan embroncs e clis,   5
   si que chans ni flors d'albespis
   no·m platz plus que l'iverns gelatz.

2. Ben tenc lo Seignor per verai
   per q'ieu veirai l'amor de loing,
   mas per un ben qe m'en eschai   10
   n'ai dos mals, car tant m'es de loing;
   ai! car me fos lai pelleris,
   si que mos fustz e mos tapis
   fos pels sieus bels oills remiratz!

3. Be·m parra jois qan li qerrai,   15
   per amor Dieu, l'alberc de loing;
   e s'a lieis platz, albergarai
   pres de lieis, si be·m sui de loing;
   adoncs parra·l parlamens fis,
   qand drutz loindas er tant vezis   20
   c'ab bels digz jauzira solatz.

4. Iratz e gauzens m'en partrai,
   qan veirai cest'amor de loing;
   mas non sai coras la veirai,
   car trop son nostras terras loing;   25
   assatz hi a portz e camis,
   e per aisso no·n sui devis...
   mas tot sia cum a Dieu platz!

Love Song

6.

1. When the days are long in May
   I love the sweet song of distant birds,
   And when I have left that place
   I remember a distant love:
   I am burdened and bowed down with desire,   5
   So that neither song nor hawthorn flower
   Pleases me more than icy winter.

2. I consider true the Lord[1]
   By whom I shall see this distant love;
   But for one good thing that happens to me   10
   I get two misfortunes, for she is so distant;
   Ah! how I wish I were a pilgrim there,
   So that my staff and my cloak
   Might be seen by her beautiful eyes!

3. It will be a joy for me when I seek it,   15
   For the love of God, that distant shelter;
   And if it please her, I shall lodge
   Near her, though I am from a distance;
   Then the meeting[2] will seem excellent,
   When this distant lover is so near   20
   That in lovely talk he will enjoy her company.

4. Sad and happy I shall leave,
   After I see this distant love;
   But I do not know when I shall ever see her,
   For our lands are too distant.   25
   There are plenty of ports and roads,
   Yet I cannot guess about the future...[3]
   But let things be as God pleases!

5. Ja mais d'amor no·m gauzirai
   si no·m gau d'est'amor de loing,   30
   que gensor ni meillor non sai
   vas nuilla part, ni pres ni loing;
   tant es sos pretz verais e fis
   qe lai el renc dels Sarrazis
   fos eu per lieis chaitius clamatz.   35

6. Dieus qui fetz tot cant ve ni vai,
   e formet cest'amor de loing,
   mi don poder, que·l cor eu n'ai,
   q'en breu veia l'amor de loing,
   veraiamen en locs aizis,   40
   si que la cambra e·l jardis
   mi resembles totz temps palatz.

7. Ver ditz qui m'apella lechai
   ni desiron d'amor de loing,
   car nuills autre jois tant no·m plai   45
   cum gauzimens d'amor de loing;
   mas so q'eu vuoill m'es tan taïs
   q'enaissi·m fadet mos pairis
   q'ieu ames e non fos amatz.

8. Mas so q'ieu vuoill m'es tan taïs: 50
   toz sia mauditz lo pairis
   qe·m fadet q'ieu non fos amatz!

1. Lai can MM^{a}R   5. Venc de t. E   6. Si c'auzels ni E
7. Val(on)(plus, mais)(qu', qan, com) CMM^{a}RSS^{g}ae^b; li vert(z)
IK   9. Que formet (fermet C) sest' CR; senyor de loyn M^a
11. Val dos a; .c. mals M^a; si be·m soi EIKRS^g 12 A! con
fora dreigs EIKS^g; (car, qe) no suy Ca   14. Sion per sos
h. S^g 15. p. iocs A   16. l'amor (l'amar E) de l. BE;
l'ostal CMM^{a}SS^{g}ae^b 19. Aqest er doutz p. a   20. es tan
v. CM^{a}e^b; sera v. SS^{g}a   21. C'ab cortes (ginh jauzis C;
joi jatz bel S^g; jeyns jau bel M^{a}e^b; ditz e bel a) CM^{a}S^{g}ae^b;
digz *lacking in* B; gauzirai s. AB; et a gai s. S   22. I. e
(dolens CM^{a}RSe^b; marritz MS^g) CMM^{a}RSS^{g}e^b 23. S'ieu no vey
sest' CSe^b; ja (la) vey (est') MM^{a}Ra; (ja, ben) remir ES^g
26. E tant i a E; maintz i a a; pas e c. CMM^{a}RSe^b 27. Per
q'ieu non puesc esser d. (vezins S) MS   28. a lieys p. Ce^b
29. Ja mais, amors R; Io d'autr'amor a; guizarai A   30. Tro

5. I shall never enjoy love
   If I do not enjoy this distant love,   30
   For I know none better or more noble
   Anywhere, either near or far;
   Her distinction is so true and fine
   That there in the Saracens' kingdom
   I would be proclaimed a captive for her.   35

6. God who made all that comes and goes,
   And created this distant love,
   Give me the strength, for I have the courage,
   Soon to see the distant love,
   Truly, in convenient places,   40
   So that the room and the garden
   May always seem a palace to me.

7. Whoever calls me greedy and desirous
   Of a distant love speaks the truth,
   For no other enjoyment pleases me as much   45
   As does the enjoyment of a distant love;
   But what I want is so kept from me,
   For so my godfather fixed my fate[4]
   That I should love and not be loved.

8. But what I want is so kept from me;   50
   Cursed be the godfather
   Who fixed my fate so that I should not be loved!

[1]"Lord" might also be read with lower case *l*, and refer to a secular lord; thus "I consider him a true lord..."; see Textual Notes.
[2]*parlamens* may also be "conversation."
[3]It is also possible that *devis* means "decided" here.
[4]For Jaufre's "godfather" see Textual Notes.

veya est' M^a 32. Ni cay ni lay ni p. M^a 33. (Car, Qe) tan (pareys son p. M^aRe^b; es sos bos p. M) sobris MM^aRe^b; p. ricx e sobris C; p. gais e fins S; E es tant sos ric p. auzitz a 35. ab lieys Ra 37. fermet BM; nostr'amor DIKS^g 38. pos talent n'ai S 39. remir (cest') a. DEIKSS^gae^b; on jauzisca d' M 40. loncs a. A; en tal (tals M) (assais D; jauzis E; aisis IKMS^g) DEIKMS^g; in palazins S 42. Me fos tan pres come longaz S; maisos e p. DEIK; novels p. Ce^b 44. deziros CMe^b; d'amon A 45. Qar neguna res M; autr' amor R 47. (50). m'es es aital R.

Textual Notes

MANUSCRIPTS

A - Rome, Bibl. Vaticana, lat. 5232 (13th c., Italy)
B - Paris, Bibl. Nationale, fr. 1592 (13th c., Italy (Jeanroy)
    or S. France (Brunel))
C - Paris, Bibl. Nationale, fr. 856 (14th c., S. France)
D - Modena, Bibl. Estense, R.4.4, Estero 45 (13th and 14th
    cc., Italy)
E - Paris, Bibl. Nationale, fr. 1749 (14th c., S. France)
I - Paris, Bibl. Nationale, fr. 854 (13th c., Italy)
K - Paris, Bibl. Nationale, fr. 12473 (13th c., Italy)
L - Rome, Bibl. Vaticana, lat. 3206 (14th c., Italy)
M - Paris, Bibl. Nationale, fr. 12474 (14th c., Italy)
M^a - Madrid, Academia de la Historia, 9.24.6/4579, No. 3 (14th
    c., Catalonia)
N^2 - Berlin, Staatsbibliothek, Phillipps 1910 (16th c., Italy)
R - Paris, Bibl. Nationale, fr. 22543 (14th c., S. France)
S - Oxford, Bodleian Library, Douce 269 (13th c., Italy)
S^g - Barcelona, Bibl. Central de la Disputación Provincial de
    Barcelona, 146 (14th c., Catalonia)
U - Florence, Bibl. Laurenziana, plut. XLI, cod. 43 (14th c.,
    Italy)
W - Paris, Bibl. Nationale, fr. 844 (13th c., N. France)
X - Paris, Bibl. Nationale, fr. 20050 (13th c., N. France)
a - Modena, Bibl. Estense, Campori, App. 426, 427, 494, N.8.4
    11-13 (16th c. Italian copy of a (probably) early 14th. c.
    MS written by the S. French scribe Bernart Amoros)
b - Rome, Bibl. Vaticana, lat. 4087 (part 1, which contains
    poems by Jaufre, is an 18th c. Italian copy of an earlier MS)
$e^{(b,g,3)}$ - Rome, Bibl. Vaticana, Barb. lat. 3965 (18th c. Italy,
    from several earlier sources)
h - Bern, Bibl. Municipale, 389 (13th c., N. France)
α - MSS of the *Breviari d'Amor* of Matfre Ermengau (see ed. of
    P.T. Ricketts)
ε - MS of *Guillaume de Dôle*, Rome, Bibl. Vaticana, Reg. lat 1725
    (13th c., N. France)

1. PRO AI DEL CHAN ESSENHADORS

(Pillet-Carstens 262.4)

Manuscripts: C, fol. 215r; e^3, pp. 190-92. *Base:* C (1-4, 6), e^3 (5, 7).
Attributions to others: None.
Major editions: Stimming, No. 3, p. 47; Monaci, No. 4, p. 6; Jeanroy, No. 3, p. 6; Casella, No. 4, p. 56; Battaglia, No. 4, p. 20; Pickens, No. 3, p. 138.
Structure: 7 8-line stanzas, all with the same rhymes (*coblas unissonans*); stanza order in C: 12346; in e^3: 1234567.
Meter and rhyme: 8 ababccde.

10. *bordeitz:* Jeanroy, following Monaci and e^3, emends to *burdens,* adj., "qui folâtrent"; our text agrees with Stimming; Suchier (1874) prefers *burdens*; Bertoni (1915) follows Stimming, and translates "toy" (cf. mod. Prov. *bourdet*; Mistral, *Tresor dou Felibrige,* I, 334).

13. *tot aitau:* Jeanroy prints *tot'aitau*; we follow Stimming and Monaci in taking *tot aitau* as an invariable formulaic phrase.

15. *sen trop soen marrir:* Stimming and Monaci print the MSS' reading *suy trop soen marritz*; we follow Jeanroy's emendation, since a rhyme-word in *-ir* is required.

16. *non ai:* Jeanroy prints *no n'ai*, but the antecedent of *n'* is somewhat dubious; we follow Stimming.

20. *enantitz:* Monaci prints e^3's *enaizitz*.

26. The phrase *sos joys* is taken here, following Bertoni (1915), as a formula similar to *sos cors*, syntactically equivalent to *elha*. Monaci prints e^3's *sest joi*.

37, 38. *amor; mal; cal:* Jeanroy adopts Stimming's emendations *amors, mau, cau*; none is necessary; in *mal* and *cal* the *-al* spelling need not affect pronunciation.

42. *e·l dia:* Stimming prints *el dia*; Jeanroy prints *et dia*, but here is not followed by Casella, whose text we follow.

43. *socors:* Stimming and Monaci print the MSS' reading *son cors* and are followed by Casella; we adopt Jeanroy's emendation since it is necessary for the rhyme in close *-ors*.

45. *fa·s elha:* Stimming prints *fas elha*; we follow with a slight change Jeanroy's *fa s'elha*.

50. *ieu au lieis:* Jeanroy emends to *non ai lieis*; our

text agrees with Stimming, following e^3. Jeanroy adopted Stimming's emendation of *luec aizit*, and we follow this for the rhyme. Topsfield (1975), p. 52, notes the contrast between *luecs aizitz* and *greu logau* in line 14.

52. *que sol baizar:* Jeanroy emends to *qu'us sols baizars;* he also adopts Stimming's emendation of *escarit* for the rhyme, and we follow this latter.

53. *lo cor:* Stimming follows e^3's *quel cor*.

54. *per:* Jeanroy emends to *pro*, which is not necessary; *per* may be taken here as an adverb of intensity.

2. BELHS M'ES L'ESTIUS E·L TEMPS FLORITZ

(Pillet-Carstens 262.1)

Manuscripts: C, fol. 214v; e^3, pp. 174-78. *Base:* C (1-6), e^3 (7-8).

Attributions to others: None.

Major editions: Stimming, No. 4, p. 49; Monaci, No. 5, p. 8; Jeanroy, No. 4, p. 9; Casella, No. 5, p. 62; Battaglia, No. 5, p. 124; Pickens, No. 4, p. 144.

Structure: Stanza-pairs (7-line stanzas) with the same rhymes alternating with stanza-pairs with the same rhymes shifted, the last three lines with the same rhymes in all stanzas (*coblas doblas*); stanza order in C: 123456; in e^3: 12345678.

Meter and rhyme: 1-2, 5-6: 8 abbaccd; 3-4, 7-8: 8 baabccd.

20. *passat ai:* Monaci prints e^3's *passatz sui*.

23. *totz selhs:* Jeanroy prints *tug silh*, following e^3 and Monaci.

25. *lhor:* Jeanroy prints *lor*.

29. *escharzitz:* Jeanroy emends to *encharzitz*, from *encharzir*, "render dearer, more valuable"; Stimming emends to *escharitz*, from *escharir*, "to accord, destine"; but the MS reading from *s'escharzir*, "to separate oneself," printed by Monaci, accords with Jaufre's theme of separation from the *turmen* and the *fol fais*.

31. *tan lunhatz:* Bertoni (1915) proposes *tan banhatz*, "bathed," a possibility which is approved, but not adopted, by Jeanroy.

32. *no·n sia:* Stimming prints *non sia*; here the pronoun ·n is necessary to link *sals* and *gueritz* to *amor*.

35. *fin'amor:* Stimming prints *fin'amor*, but takes it to be the direct object of *home*, leaving unexplained why he does not print *homs*, which would be required in the case system. In any event, *fin'amor* as subject need not be emended.

46. For interpretations of *fraire* and *seror*, e.g., among others, the twin components of the personality in medieval alchemy, see Topsfield (1975), p. 59 and note 13.
47. *nuills*: Jeanroy emends to *nulhs*.
51. *lurs*: We follow Jeanroy, who emends to *lur*, which Anglade, *Grammaire*, p. 252, says "remains invariable in the classic period."
52. *vueill*: Jeanroy emends to *vuelh*. Note subjunctive *sia*, governed by *vueill*, without connecting *que*.
55. *rics*: Jeanroy emends to *ric*.
56. *fol fais*: Cf. Marcabru's *Ans que·l terminis verdei*, 21, and Cercamon, 8.47.

3. NO SAP CHANTAR QUI SO NON DI

(Pillet-Carstens 262.3)

Manuscripts: C, fol. 215r-v; E, p. 150; M, fol. 166r; R, fol. 63r; a, pp. 458-59; b, fol. 5r-6v; e, pp. 192-96 (e^g and e^3); α, 29417-22. *Base:* E (last two stanzas, defective in E owing to a removed initial, supplied from e^3).

Attributions to others: a (Bernart Marti).

Major editions: Stimming, No. 6, p. 53; Monaci, No. 1, p. 3; Jeanroy, No. 6, p. 16; Casella, No. 1, p. 40; Battaglia, No. 1, p. 114; Pickens, No. 6, p. 215.

Structure: 6 6-line stanzas plus 1 tornada, all with the same rhymes (*coblas unissonans*); stanza order in C: 1 2(7-8)-S-5(29-30) 3(13-14)-U 4(19-20)-T-W YZ67 (lettered stanzas, following Pickens, found below); in Ee^3: 1234567; in Me^g: 1 2(7-8)-S-5(29-30) 4(19-20)-T 6; in R: 1 2(7-10)-5(29-30) 34 67; in a: 12Q5 3(13-14)-R 467.

Meter and rhyme: 8 abbaab + ab.

Music: R (see Musical Appendix).
lines peculiar to C

S. ni nulha res ta mal no·m fa
   quo so qu'anc de mos huelhs no vi

U. s'em breu merce no·l pren de mi
   e anc hom tan gen no mori
   ab tan dous mal ni no·n s'escha

T. a la belha que mon cor a
   on mey voler fan dreg cami

W. e pot ben dir s'aman m'auci
   que mais tan fizel non aura

Y. Un'amor lonhdana m'auci
   e·l dous dezirs propdas m'esta
   e quan m'albir qu'ieu me n'an la
   en forma d'un bon pellegri
   mey voler son siey anc issi
   de ma mort qu'estiers no sera

Z. Peironet, passa riu; di li
   que mos cors a lieys passara,
   e si li platz, alberguar m'a
   per que·l parlamen sera fi;
   mal me faderon mey pairi
   s'amors m'auci per lieys que m'a

lines peculiar to Me^g

S. qar nuilha res tan mal no·m fa
   con co qez anc dels hueilhs non vi

T. on li bella si dorm, e ja
   mei dezir fan lai lur cami
   mei suspir son sei assasi
   de l'amor no sai qo·m penra (a a M)

lines peculiar to a

R. senes pro qe ja no n'aura

Q. E si tan fai qe zo devi
   ma domna cossi m'amara
   pos messatgiers lai non ira
   ni eu m'en metrai el cami;
   e s'anc per leis null mal suffri,
   ja per mon grat non o sabra

    Compare the treatment of love in this song with Cercamon No. 6. This is the only song for which Jeanroy did not use C as a base. Here he uses E, and we follow him. Note below, however, his deviations from E's text and spelling.
    1. *qui so:* Monaci and Casella print MRe^g's *qui·l so*.
    2. *qui motz:* Monaci and Casella print MRe^g's *qui·ls motz*.
    5. *aisi:* Jeanroy prints *aissi*.
    6, 12, 18, 24, 30, 36, 38. Monaci and Jeanroy print M's *a a* after each stanza-final rhyme word; see Musical Appendix.
    8. *ja no·m veira:* Stimming prints *no veirai ja*, follow-

157

ing CMe^g.
   9. *a:* Jeanroy prints *ha*.
   10. *de cela que:* Stimming prints *aissella*; Jeanroy prints *qu'ieu anc*.
   11-12. Stimming prints 29-30 here, following CMRe^g.
   12. *e:* Stimming prints *ni*.
   13. *Colps:* Stimming prints *Colp*.
   17. *nuill:* Casella prints *nulhs*.
   19. *suau:* We follow Jeanroy in rejecting Ee^3's *soven*, printed by Stimming and Monaci, which makes little sense in this context, and in printing C's reading.
   23. *mais:* Monaci and Jeanroy print *e*, following a; Stimming and Monaci print R's *mais* (Monaci: *e*) *quan* (*cant* R) *mi ressit lo mati*. Ee^3's *ho* makes little sense as it stands, and we follow Stimming in adopting *mais*.
   25-30. Compare this stanza with William IX's *Farai un vers de dreit nien*, especially 25-36.
   29-30. Stimming prints 11-12 here, following CMRe^g.
   30. *so:* Jeanroy prints *s'o*, but the extra particle *s'* is not necessary. We follow Jeanroy in adopting CMe^g's *so fara* for Ee^3's *mi veira*, printed by Monaci, which appears also in line 8, but which here is redundant.
   31ff. Stimming's stanzas 6 and 7 are C's stanzas Y and Z which we have followed Jeanroy in judging apocryphal.
   31-36. Ortiz (1943) suggests that stanza Z in C beginning *Peironet passa·l riu* (see above) was later interpolated by a jongleur named Peironet.
   31. *anc no·l failli:* Jeanroy emends to *qu'anc no·i falhi*; Stimming prints R's *can no·i f*.
   34. *gart no·l franha ni no·l:* Jeanroy emends to *gart se no·l franha ni·l*; Stimming prints *no·l falha*, following R.
   35. *e vueill l'auja en Caersi:* The subjunctive *auja* is here governed by the indicative *vueill* without connecting *que*; cf. 2.52. Jeanroy emends to *car si l'auran en Caerci*; Stimming prints CMRe^g's *si l'auzon*.
   37-38. Suchier (1874) suggests that these lines allude to the Second Crusade, and that *hi* refers to the Holy Land, where Bertrand and Alphonse-Jourdain will perform memorable deeds; Crescini (1890) disputes this. Indeed, taking the Holy Land as antecedent of *hi* seems forced; *hi* more naturally takes as antecedents *Caersi* and *Tolza*, already mentioned in the stanza. Ortiz (1909) proposes emending *lo vers* to *lo sos*, and *calqe re* to *casqus motz*.

4. QAN LO RIUS DE LA FONTANA

(Pillet-Carstens 262.6)

Manuscripts: A, fol. 127v; B, fol. 77v; C, fol. 214r; D, fol. 88r; E, p. 149; I, fol. 122r; K, fols. 107v-108r; M, fol. 165v; R, fol. 63v; S, pp. 183-84; S^g, fol. 108r-v; U, fol. 126v; a, pp. 278-79; b, fol. 6v; e^b, pp. 180-82; X, fol. 149v; h, part 2, fol. 1r. *Base:* A (transcribed in Pakscher and De Lollis (1891), 396).

Attributions to others: a (Guilhem de Cabestanh), X (anon.), h (anon.).

Major editions: Stimming, No. 2, p. 44; Monaci, No. 3, p. 5; Jeanroy, No. 2, p. 3; Casella, No. 2, p. 46; Battaglia, No. 2, p. 116; Pickens, No. 2, p. 88.

Structure: A stanza-pair (7-line stanzas) with the same rhymes followed by a stanza-pair with the same rhymes shifted (*coblas doblas*), the last stanza identical to the second pair, and the last line of each stanza with the same rhyme throughout; stanza order in ABDEIK: 12345; in CR: 1234D5 (lettered stanzas, following Pickens, are found below); in M: 1234F5; in S: 1234; in S^g: 12345; in U: 123DH F-4(26-28); in a: 1234 F-4(22-25) K5; in b: 2(8-11) G; in e^b: 1234G5; in X: 1 2(8-10)-J; in h: 1 2(8-10)-J K L-3(17-21) M.

Meter and rhyme: 1, 2: 8a' 7b 8c' 7d 8a' 8c' 8e'; 3, 4, 5: 8c' 7d 8a' 7b 8c' 8a' 8e'.

Music: R (see Musical Appendix).

lines peculiar to CR (base C)

D. Quan pensar m'en fai aizina
   adoncs la bays e l'acol
   mas pueys torn en revolina
   per que·m n'espert e n'aflam
   quar so que floris non grana
   lo joy que mi n'ataÿna
   tot mos cujatz afaitanha.

lines peculiar to M

F. Si·n sui de lonja taïna
   e mais seinha no·n susfrainh
   co dis li gen anciana
   q'ab sufrir venz savis fol
   q'ades s'en ven de rabina
   mas ieu aten causa vana
   q'ailhor remanc en la fainha.

lines peculiar to U

D. Sem pensier la·m fai proçana
   ladoncs la bais e l'acol
   mais pois dinz Mirimolina
   per q'eu m'esperc e aflam
   qar sai si flors ni grana
   le joi q'era de ço camina
   tro qu'a mos guabs a fach tangna.

H. Sa contenensa es soldana
   qe joi mi grup'e m'afoilh
   e non fai amor vizina
   q'en abanz non cant q'eu bram
   tan desir l'amor de cusana
   cui jois e jovens aclina
   cum fos lai en terra straigna.

F. Trop soi de loinga traïna
   qe messatgiers non fraing
   e diz la gent anciana
   qe sufrent venz savi fol

lines peculiar to a

F. qe sobrevoler la·m tol
   plus tost s'en vai de rabina
   et eu son cun causa vana
   las! qi remaing en la fagna.

K. Ben agra bona setmana
   qe de leis agues son vol
   qe duguessa ni regina
   non es qi de leis no·s clam
   boc'ha vermeilla cun grana
   e sembla roza d'espina
   mesclad'ab neu de montagna.

lines peculiar to e^b (first two lines also in b)

G. Entre Grec e Trasmontana
   volgr'esser dins el mar
   et agues can e traïna
   ab que m'anes deportar
   fuec e lenha e sertana

e pron peison per cozinar
e midons per companha.

the French version in Xh (base h)

1. Kant li rus de la fontaine
    renclarsist si come solt,
    ke naist la flour aglentainne,
    et roisignor chante el ro,
    volv e i refraint et aplaigne   5
    son douls chanteir et afine,
    drois es ke li miens refraigne.

2. Amors de terre lointainne,
    por vos tous li cors me dolt,
    e non peuc troveir messine   10
    s'on ne l'ait per vo confort
    e retrait d'amor altaigne
    en vergier ou sor gaudainne,
    tail desir ai de compaigne.

3. Moult auroit bone semainne   15
    ki de li auroit son vol,
    c'ains contesse ne Rodainne
    non ot tant avenant cors:
    bouche ait vermoille com grainne
    et semble roze en espaine,   20
    blanche est com noix de montaigne.

4. Pues ke tout mi fait lonsainne,
    no meiravis s'on es fol,
    k'ains si belle Crestiainne
    ne fut, ne Deuz ne la volt,   25
    Judee ne Sarazainne:
    bien seroit paus del mainne
    [ki] tient de s'amor gadainne.

5. Ensi com cottidienne
    com chascuns die et retor,   30
    lou cors ke per sumelainne
    ait tenue en son redol
    (ensi amors mi demainne),
    et tient pres de sai saixaine
    et paist de dousor prochainne.   35

2. com fait s. X 3. e peirt la f. X 4. el rols X 7. li

amens X   12-13. et nonbra d'amor sodainne / el v. o so gor-
dainne X   12. retraut h   14. o desirair de c. X   15-36. *lacking in* X   28. mi t. h   35. et paist et paist h

 11. *si non vau al sieu:* Jeanroy emends to *si non au vostre r.*, following Crescini (1890) and Paris (1893); our text agrees with Stimming, Monaci and Casella.
 14. *desirada:* Topsfield (1975), p. 51 (and note 6), says that this word "has associations with Christ," for whom *desiratus* is found as a name in medieval Latin.
 15. *Pois del tot:* Jeanroy prints *Pus totz jorns*, following CMSUe[b].
 18. *que Dieus:* Jeanroy emends to *ni Dieus*.
 20. *et es ben:* Jeanroy prints C's *ben es selh*.
 21. The adjectives *Crestiana, Juzeva, Sarrazina*, and the noun *manna* "cannot fail," says Topsfield (1975), p. 51, "to evoke the Holy Land."
 26. For the possiblity of *espina* as St. Paul's thorn see Lefèvre (1966).
 29-35. Cocito (1969) suggests that this stanza was added by a later jongleur, and refers to events concerning a later Hugh the Swarthy which took place at the beginning of the thirteenth century.
 30. *que chantam:* This is the reading of DIKS[g], and has been adopted for the rhyme, following Jeanroy.
 31. *plan et en lenga:* Jeanroy prints CEMa's *en plana lengua*.
 32. *Fillol:* Ortiz (1943) suggests that *Fillol* is the reference of *per lui* in line 35, and that the stanza is an interpolation by a jongleur named Fillol.
 33. *bon m'es:* Jeanroy prints *bo·m sap*, following CMe[b].
 34-35. ABC's rhyme words *Bretaigna* (34) and *Guianna* (35) have been reversed, following Jeanroy, to conform to the rhyme-scheme.
 34. Frank (1942) mentions that Louis VII announced his crusading intentions at Bourges, capital of Berry, possibly explaining the appearance of *Beiriu* here, which would be relevant to Hugh's departure on crusade.
 35. *s'esgau per lui:* Stimming prints *per leis*; Jeanroy, following Crescini's (1890) suggestion, prints *per lui*. Frank (1942) argues for *per leis*, taking *leis* as referring to the love of the Holy Land. Monaci (1893) held, however, that *leis* refers to Eleanor of Aquitaine. Ortiz chose *per lui*; see above, note 32. The people mentioned in the stanza may simply be rejoicing for Hugh's honor, and he may have been on crusade at the time. As for the other names in the stanza, it should be remembered that they are formulaic, and mean "all the surrounding regions," and that Jaufre was working under the con-

straints of rhyme, which explains the appearance of some regions and not others.

5. QUAN LO ROSSINHOLS EL FOLLOS

(Pillet-Carstens 262.6)

Manuscripts: A, fol. 127r; B, fols. 76v-77r; C, fol. 214r-v; D, fol. 88r; E, pp. 149-50; I, fol. 122r; K, fol. 108r; M, fol. 166r-v; N^2, fol. 19r; R, fol. 63v; S^g, fol. 108v; a, p. 499; e^g, pp. 178-80. *Base:* C.
Attributions to others: None.
Major editions: Stimming, No. 1, p. 41; Monaci, No. 7, p. 10; Jeanroy, No. 1, p. 1; Casella, No. 6, p. 68; Battaglia, No. 6, p. 127; Pickens, No. 1, p. 61.
Structure: 6 7-line stanzas, all with the same rhymes (*coblas unissonans*); stanza order in CE: 123456; in R: 12345; in $ABDIKN^2S^g$: 14AB5 (A and B, following Pickens, are found below); in Me^g: 14AB56; in a: 154B.
Meter and rhyme: 8 ababbc'd.
Music: R (see Musical Appendix).

lines peculiar to $ABDIKN^2S^gMae^g$ (base A)

A. De tal dompna sui cobeitos
    a cui non aus dir mon talen;
    anz qan remire sas faissos,
    totz lo cors m'en vai esperden;
    et aurai ja tant d'ardimen
    que l'aus dir per sieu mi teigna,
    puois d'als no·il aus merce querrer.

B. A! cum son siei dich amoros,
    e siei faich son doutz e plazen;
    c'anc non nasqet sai entre nos
    neguna c'aia·l cors tant gen:
    grail'es e fresca ab cor plazen,
    e non cre gensser s'enseigna,
    ni no·n vi hom ab tant plazer.

20. que per A; qe patz m'en t. M; mainteinha e^g 21. p. (eu) no·il aus AB   22. saboros S^gMe^g; enveios a   23. bon fach (bel dig a) fin e valen Me^ga 25. tan bella de neguna gen Me^g; sa pars segon mon escien a   26. cors a g. dolgat plazen Me^g; qe·l cors a blanc e gai e gen a   27. si s. Me^g; per q'ieu

163

non cug tam bella regna a   28. ni anc homs son la poc vezer
Me[g]; ni anc qant lo pogues vezer a.

   6. que·y renha: Jeanroy prints que renha.
   8. D'un'amistat: Jeanroy's text reads D'un amistat,
which may be a misprint; we follow Stengel's and Casella's D'un'.
   10. c'or: Casella takes joya to be the antecedent of c'.
   14. e s'amors: Stimming prints es s'amors, following R.
   18. joyos, jauzen: Jeanroy's conjecture is jauzitz
jauzen.
   24. reüsos: Stimming prints reversos, following C,
which we ascribe uniquely to C's copyist.
   25. que lay·s n'an: Stimming prints qu'ella m'an, following ABDIKN[2]RS[g]; Jeanroy emends to qu'ela·s n'an.
   26. cor: Jeanroy prints vai, following CMEe[g].
   27. er que lai: Jeanroy emends to er qu'oimais.
   28. s'amors no la·m fai remaner: CE's s'ilha no·s vol
aretener (aremaner E) has the appearance of a lectio facilior,
and we follow Jeanroy in printing the better reading of ABDIK
MN[2]RS[g]e[g]. a's s'ab merce suggests a corruption of s'amors.
   29ff. Stimming's stanzas 5 and 6 are ABDIKMN[2]Sge[g]'s
stanzas A and B.
   29. alegres: Jeanroy prints alegre·m, following DEIKN[2]
RS[g]a; our text agrees with Stimming.
   31. en tant: Casella prints suy d'aitant.
   33-35. CE's reading mas pero per mon Bon Guiren...m'es
ops aparcer mon voler, while a satisfactory reading, has the
appearance of a lectio facilior, and goes against most of the
manuscripts; hence we have followed Jeanroy.
   33. Bon Guiren: Cravayat argues that the "Good Protect-
or" is William VI Taillefer, Count of Angoulême; see Life of
the Author. Casella prints bon guiren, following Monaci.
   36-42. Cf. Cercamon 8, stanza 8.
   38. ja mais sia: Stimming prints sia jamais.
   41. qui Jhesus: Stimming prints cui J.; our text agrees
with Jeanroy's spelling, but Jeanroy, as does Stimming, takes
Jhesus to be the subject of essenha. The phrase tener escola
means "to hold, conduct (a) school"; this makes it natural to
take Jhesus as object of essenha. For tener escola taken as
meaning "to follow a (certain) path or course of action,"
from escola, "group, body of followers," thus opening the
possibility of Jhesus as subject of essenha, see Jeanroy in
Romania, 41, 418, note 3. Jeanroy's interpretation of our
passage, relegated to a note, is speculative.

6. LANQAN LI JORN SON LONC EN MAI

(Pillet-Carstens 262.2)

Manuscripts: A, fol. 127r-v; B, fol. 77r-v; C, fols. 214v-215r; D, fol. 88r-v; E, p. 149; I, fols. 121v-122r; K, fol. 107v; M, fol. 165r-v; M^a, fol. 4r-v; R, fol. 63r-v; S, pp. 182-83; S^g, fol. 108r; a, pp. 498-99; b, fol. 6v; e^b, pp. 186-90; W, fols. 189v-190r; X, fol. 81v; ε (1299-1305), fol. 75r. *Base:* A (with C's order of stanzas; transcribed in in Pakscher and De Lollis (1891), 395).
    Attributions to others: W (Gaucelm Faidit).
    Major editions: Stimming, No. 5, p. 50; Monaci, No. 2, p. 4; Jeanroy, No. 5, p. 12; Casella, No. 3, p. 50; Battaglia, No. 3, p. 118; Pickens, No. 5, p. 150.
    Structure: 7 7-line stanzas plus 1 tornada, all with the same rhymes (*coblas unissonans*); order of stanzas in AB: 154 32678; in C: 12345678; in D: 15 4(22-23)-6(38-42) 3; in EIK: 15 4(22-23)-2(10-14) 63; in M: 1634 7(43-46)-2(12-14) 5; in M^a: 163 2(8-9)-5(31-35) 5(29-30)-4(24-28) 4(22-23)-2(10-11)-7(47-49); in R: 126457; in S: 15346; in S^g: 15 4(22-23)-2(10-14) 63 7(43-44)-5(31-32)-P; in a: 1 6(36-39)-4(26-28) 235 4(22-25); in e^b: 12345 6(36-39)-7(47-49); in X: 123 5(27-30)-4(24-28); in W: 13 5(29-30)-2(10-14) 2(8-9)-5(31-35).
    Meter and rhyme: 8 ababccd + ccd.
    Music: R, W, X (see Musical Appendix).

lines peculiar to S^g

P.   car fin'amor a tan apris
     que cant troba dos amans fis
     sab ben faire d'estrains privatz

the French version in W

1.   Lan que li jor sunt lonc en may,
     m'est bel dolz chanz d'oisel de [loig],
     [e q]an me sui partis de lai
     membre [moi d'un]e amor de loig;
     vais de talens bruns et enclins,
     si que chanz ne flors d'aubespins
     non val maiz que l'ivers gelatz.

2.   Mol teg lou Segnor per verai
     per que l'en dit amor de loig,
     et per un ben que m'en eschai

ai deus maus, car trop sui de loig;
   Dex! car fusse sains pelegrins
   tan que mos fust e mos tapins
   fust de ses biauz ex remirais.

3. Ben parra jois quant li querrai
   per amors de l'hostal de loig,
   e se li plais, hebergerai
   pres de li, car trop sui de loig;
   adoncs sera parlemens fins
   quant dru lointains seront veisins:
   en corteis jois gist gens soulais.

4. Ja mais d'amors non jauzirai
   se non jauzis d'amors de loig,
   e bien sai que grieument l'aurai,
   quar trop sunt nostres terres loig;
   Dieus! tant i a pas et chemins
   que griement en serai siasins;
   or seit del tot si com li plais!

the French version in X

1. Lan qant li jor sont lonc en mai
   m'est bel del chant d'auziaus de long,
   e qant me sui partiz de lai
   membre moi d'une amor de long;
   vains de talant bruns et enclin
   si que chant ne flors d'aubespin
   non mi vaut mais qu'ivers jalaiz.

2. Bien aurai joi qant li querrai
   por amor Dieu l'ostal de long,
   e se li plaist, s'erbergerai
   pres de li, que trop sui de long;
   adons sera parlemanz fins
   quant dru lontan sont pres voisin:
   q'en corteis gen gist beaus solaz.

3. Ja mais d'amor non jauzirai
   s'eu non jauzis d'amor de long;
   qant por un ben qui m'en eschai
   n'ai dous mals que trop sui de long;
   he las! que non fui palerin,
   si que mos fuz et mos tapin
   fous de ses bels euz remiraz!

4. Celui Seignor teng por verai
   qui fait jauzir d'amor de long;
   plus bele ne gencor ne sai
   negune part ne pres ne long;
   tant aim son douz vis et son ris
   ke lonz en terre es Sarrazin
   volgre por li chaidis clamar.

5. vains   14. geu gist   22. pir v.

the French version in ε

1. Lorsque li jor sont lonc en mai
   m'es biaus doz chant d'oisel de lonc,
   et quant me sui partiz de la,
   menbre mi d'une amor de lonc;
   vois de ca gens bruns et enduis,
   si que chans ne flors d'aubespin
   ne mi val ne cu'ivers gelas.

    8. Bertoni (1915) argues for a small *s* in *lo senhor*; he is followed by Lewent (1961).
    16. *alberc*: Lejeune (1959) argues for *amor*.
    21. *c'ab bels digz jauzira solatz*: Burger (1966) proposes C's *qu'ab cortes ginh jauzis solatz*; Jeanroy's text bears the probable misprint *et tan vezis*; Lejeune (1959) emends to *jauzirai·s*.
    23. *qan veirai cest'*: Jeanroy prints MM[a]Ra's *s'ieu ja la vey*; our text agrees with Stimming. Lejeune (1959) prints *cest* (for *cest'*), which may be a misprint.
    26. *portz*: Jeanroy prints *pas*, following CMM[a]RSe[b].
    27. For *devis*, cf. Cercamon 3.33.
    37. *formet*: Lejeune prints *fermet*, "fixed."
    39. *q'en breu veia l'*: Jeanroy emends to *qu'ieu veya sest'*; our text agrees with Stimming.
    40. *en locs*: Jeanroy prints DEIKMS[g]'s *en tal(s)*; our text agrees with Stimming.
    47, 50. *tan taïs*: Stimming prints *tant ahis*, and is followed by Lejeune. Jeanroy emends to *m'es atahis*, and takes *atahis* to be a masculine form of *atahina*. However, given the form *taïn*, "delay," (Levy, *PD*, p. 356), from Germ. *taheins*, "diversion," the form *ahis* seems indefensible; see *FEW*, 17, 291, and *Donatz Proensals*, ed. J.H. Marshall, 813: *ataïnar*, "to impede." *taïs* is thus a participle meaning "kept from, withheld."
    48, 51. *pairis*: Lejeune takes Jaufre to be referring to William IX of Aquitaine.

GLOSSARY OF SPECIAL WORDS

(See note to Cercamon glossary)

AIGLENTINA   wild rose   4.3
AVENTUROS   fortunate   5.31
BATESTAU   dispute   1.46
BIAIS   3rd sing. pres. subj. of *biaisar*, to slant, lean   2.49
BORDEITZ   games   1.10 (TN)
COBITZ   past part. of *cobir*, to accord   2.4
CORS (LO)   swiftly   1.41
CORS (MOS, SOS)   idiom functioning as personal pronoun   1.33, 2.40, 44, 3.22, (4.9), 4.22, 5.32
DEPARTIR   to settle (a dispute)   1.47
DESDITZ   3rd sing. pres. ind. of *desdire*, to deny, refuse   2.45
DESVA   3rd sing. pres. ind. of *dezanar*, to escape   3.24
DEVIS   one who can guess about or see into the future, know about   6.27
ENBRONCS   dejected   6.5
ESCARIT[Z] (PER)   singled out, hence "a single..."   1.52
ESCHAI   3rd sing. pres. ind. of *eschazer*, to happen (to)   6.10
ESCHARZITZ (M'EN SUI)   past part. of *s'escharzir*, to depart from, separate oneself from   2.29 (TN)
ESCOLA (TENER)   to hold, conduct (a) school   5.42 (TN)
FADET   3rd sing. pret. of *fadar*, to fix someone's fate   6.48, 52
FUSTZ   pilgrim's staff   6.13
GART   help, attention   1.56
JAUZIR   (sometimes reflexive) to gladden; to enjoy (sexually)   1.7, 3.25, 26, 5.18, 6.21; see also *jauzens* 1.12, 48, 5.3, 18, 32, 6.22, 29; *jauzitz* 1.12, 2.8; *jauzimen* 1.40, 2.5, 6.46
LECHAI   greedy   6.43
PARLAMENS   meeting; conversation   6.19 (fn)
PER   variant of *pro*, much, a lot   1.54
PIMPAS   pipes, flutes   1.9
PREZEN   reward   2.26
PRO   many, plenty   1.1
RECLAM   call,   4.11
REVERT A MAL   3rd sing. pres. ind. of *revertar a mal*, destroy, undo   1.37
TAÏS   past part. of *taïnar*, to impede   6.47, 50 (TN)
TAPIS   pilgrim's cloak   6.13
VOUTAS   songs   1.4

INDEX OF NAMES

BEIRIU   Berry, region of France southeast of Tours, in whose capital, Bourges, Louis VII announced his intention to join the Second Crusade   4.34 (TN)
BETHLEEM   Bethlehem   5.37
BERTRANS (EN)   probably Bertrand, bastard son of Alphonse-Jourdain of Toulouse   3.36
BON GUIREN   Good Protector, possibly a veiled reference to William VI Taillefer, Count of Angoulême, cousin and suzerain of Jaufre Rudel; also possibly a nickname for Jaufre's lady   5.33 (TN)
BRETAIGNA   Brittany   4.35 (TN)
CAERSI   Quercy, region of France whose capital, Cahors, is about 60 miles north of Toulouse   3.35
DIEUS   God   2.25, 4.18, 5.37, 6.16, 28, 36
FILLOL   Godson, possibly the name of a jongleur, or a messenger   4.32 (TN)
GUIANNA   Guyenne, region of France just to the south and east of Bordeaux   4.35
HUGON BRUN   probably Hugh VII the Swarthy of Lusignan, who went on crusade in 1147   4.32
JHESUS   Jesus   5.41
PEITAVINA (GENS)   Poitevin, of the region of France surrounding, and to the west of, Poitiers   4.33
SARRAZIS   Saracens   6.34
SEIGNOR (LO)   the Lord; but see fn and TN   6.8
TOLZA (·L COMS EN)   the Count in Toulouse, i.e. Alphonse-Jourdain   3.36

INDEX OF OPENING LINES

Poem No.

Belhs m'es l'estius e·l temps floritz 2
Lanqan li jorn son lonc en mai 6
No sap chantar qui so non di 3
Pro ai del chan essenhadors 1
Quan lo rossinhols el follos 5
Qan lo rius de la fontana 4

The Music of Jaufre Rudel
by
Hendrik van der Werf

Jaufre Rudel is one of the earliest, if not the earliest, troubadour for whom the medieval sources preserve some complete melodies. Considering the sad fact that so few troubadour melodies survive--some 250 tunes for well over 2000 poems--it is quite remarkable that we have the music for four of Jaufre's six extant poems. One of them even appears in three different manuscripts and was used again by later poets. It is tempting to conclude from this that Jaufre's melodies enjoyed an extraordinary popularity during and after his lifetime. This assumption is hazardous, however, because we know next to nothing about the forces and circumstances which kept certain melodies alive but let others disappear forever.

It is equally tempting and hazardous to credit Jaufre with the invention of what is often called the *canzone* form. In this form (graphically represented as AB AB X) the first two melodic lines (A & B) are repeated for the third and fourth verses of the poem. The rest of the melody may be completely new (e.g. AB AB CD as in Song 3, or AB AB CDE as in Song 5), or it may contain some repetition (e.g. AB AB CB'D as in Song 4, or AB AB CDB as in Song 6, or MS. R's version of Song 6, AB AB A'CB). Often the texts of such songs show a similar subdivision, at least in their rhymes. For example, all four of Jaufre's songs that have been preserved with music have an *ab ab x* rhyme-scheme. Sometimes, even the syntax and content of the strophe correspond to the form of the melody and rhyme. Many troubadour and trouvère *chansons*, as well as many later songs from various countries, both monophonic and polyphonic, were fashioned in this form. Even though Jaufre is the first poet-composer who is known to have used this form, one cannot justify calling it his creation merely because we know nothing about the music of his predecessors. It would be unwise to assume that the peoples of southern France and the rest of western Europe did not have any songs before Count William of Poitou. After all, ethnomusicological research has shown that even so-called primitive tribes have their songs, and repetition of melodic and textual ideas is a common feature in many of them.

Although one should not attach great significance to the literary and musical criticism found in the medieval *vidas* and *razos*, it is easy to agree with the statement that Jaufre's songs had "good tunes." They appeal to us because they are more cohesive than most troubadour melodies, and they combine syllabic and ornate passages in well-balanced fashion. In my estimation, Jaufre's tunes are among the most attractive troubadour melodies. Unfortunately, the study of style in medieval music is not sufficiently advanced to allow a more detailed and more objective evaluation of Jaufre as a composer. For example, two rather different approaches to melodic analysis have been given by van der Werf (pp. 46-59) and Le Vot. It is dangerous, therefore, to go as far as Jean-Baptiste Beck and attribute to Jaufre an anonymously preserved *chanson* primarily because its melody resembles stylistically those assigned to him in the medieval sources (Beck, *Le Manuscrit du roi*, II, 105-6). If one were to be consistent in such an endeavor and base attributions upon melodic characteristics, one might well have to ignore all medieval assignments and conclude that the entire troubadour repertory stems from approximately half a dozen different composers.

It is true that the four melodies preserved with poems attributed to Jaufre Rudel display a certain stylistic uniformity. It is not certain, however, that all of them were composed by him. Three German and two Latin poems have been preserved with tunes which, at least in part, are related to that of Song 6. For various reasons, the relationship among them is rather complex and deserves our attention. The pertinent melodies are given here synoptically. Horst Brunner is thus far the only scholar to have given an extensive discussion of this problem (*Walther von der Vogelweide*, 54*-56*, transcriptions 82*-84*, photographic reproductions 217-22 and 293-94). Jaufre's melody survives in three manuscripts, the earliest two of which, X and W, were compiled approximately a century after his death. As usual, the three melodies differ somewhat from one another, so that all are included here. Although the Latin songs have been preserved in many manuscripts (six of which are given by Brunner), only a single version of one of them is presented here. The main justification for this restriction lies in the close similarity among their extant versions. The relation between the two Latin songs was discussed extensively by Manfred Bukofzer before their relation to Jaufre's song was known. One of them, *Ave rex gentis Anglorum miles regis angelorum* honors the English martyr St. Edmund (d. 868), king of East Anglia, whose feast was introduced into the English liturgy in the year 1013 (Bukofzer, p. 17). The earliest sources known at present for this chant, the antiphonals from Worcester and Salisbury, date from the thirteenth century. All subsequent sources are also of English origin. Thus, even if this version is the older of the Latin songs, it is unlikely that Jaufre knew this particular text.

The other Latin text, however, *Ave regina angelorum mater regis angelorum* (not to be confused with the more widely used *Ave regina caelorum ave domina angelorum*) has been found in many continental manuscripts. According to Michel Huglo, in certain churches it was sung at the conclusion of Complines on one designated day of the week ("Les livres liturgiques de la Chaise-Dieu," *Revue Bénédictine*, 87 (1977), 342). Its oldest known version (which was not known to Brunner) is a marginal addition to the late eleventh-century gradual of St. Yriex, in southern

France (Paris, Bibliothèque Nationale, latin 903, folio 162r). Its notation suggests that this version was copied in the middle of the twelfth century, that is, possibly during Jaufre's lifetime. As is almost common for southern French plain-chant manuscripts of this time, the notation has no clef; it does not even have any lines for a staff. Accordingly, it is inadvisable to present it here in transcription. The melodic contour, however, is very clear and shows beyond any doubt that, in essence, this melody is the same as the ones preserved in later and more precisely notated manuscripts. The melody included in our synoptic chart was taken from what may well be the next oldest source (Stadtbibliothek Schlettstadt 22, folio 12v, facsimile Brunner 216).

Although all of the German songs are more recent than Jaufre's, the melody preserved with Walther von der Vogelweide's crusade song must be discussed here. In general it is very closely related to Jaufre's melody, but in some respects it resembles the Latin song more closely than does Jaufre's. The other two German songs are clearly based on Walther's and can therefore be omitted from our deliberations. Ursula Aarburg, in a posthumously published article, was the first to point to the remarkable similarities between certain lines of this *Ave regina* and the melody attributed to the German poet Walther von der Vogelweide. Before that, Heinrich Husmann was the first to notice the close relations between Walther's and Jaufre's melodies.

The overall relation between the melodies for Jaufre's text and the one for Walther's poem is rather convincing, but the relation between these two and the Latin one is quite complex. The former two have seven lines of text, while the latter has six. Melodically, however, the Latin song has five distinctly different lines because, except for a few variants, the fourth line is repeated for the last verse. The other two songs, however, repeat two lines so that the total melody consists of no more than four different lines in the following form: AB AB CDB. (Certain peculiarities of the last line in MS. W are probably caused by a scribal error to be discussed shortly). In MS. R, moreover, the pitches for the fifth line are an almost literal repeat of the first melodic line transposed up a fifth. Thus, in that manuscript, Jaufre's melody consists of only three different lines (AB AB A'CB).

As the synoptic chart of all three songs shows, the B-melodies of Jaufre's and Walther's tunes are clearly related to the fourth and sixth lines of the Latin song. It is noteworthy, however, that Walther's version resembles the Latin melody more closely than it does Jaufre's. The fifth line of the Latin song appears to be related to parts of the C- and the D- melodies in

Jaufre's and Walther's songs, more or less as illustrated in the synoptic chart. For the other lines it is open to discussion whether the Latin song is related to Jaufre's and/or Walther's. The exact kinship among these melodies is not immediately apparent.

After considering several possibilities, Brunner postulates that, in all likelihood, the Latin chant was the model for Jaufre's melody. Jaufre omitted the first two lines of the *Ave regina* and began his song with an adaptation of the chant's third line, while keeping the fourth line more or less as it was. More importantly, Jaufre decided to reshape the chant's form into the *canzone* form, by using his first and second lines twice in immediate succession. Next, Jaufre expanded the rest of the melody so that the fifth line of the *Ave regina* was used for the fifth and sixth lines of his text. Approximately half a century later, Walther von der Vogelweide used Jaufre's melody for his song. Brunner gives two explanations for the fact that, in certain respects, the melody of the *Ave regina* is more closely related to Walther's than to Jaufre's. First, it is possible that Walther knew not only the Provençal, but also the Latin version of the melody. He may have taken the *canzone* form from Jaufre's song, but several melodic turns from the Latin one. Second, since more than a century lies between the composition and the preservation of Jaufre's song, it may well have been changed considerably during its long oral tradition. It is not impossible that Jaufre's own melody resembled the *Ave regina* melody more closely than any of the extant versions. Together, Brunner's postulations satisfactorily explain the complex relationship among the three songs.

Unlike Brunner, however, I do not want to rule out the possibility that Jaufre's tune was the parent of both other melodies. First, it may have been adapted for the Latin song. Repetition of the first two melodic lines, giving the total song the AB AB X form, was a favorite formal device among the troubadours. In the liturgical repertory, however, this form does not seem to have taken hold. In the troubadour repertory, additional repetition of melodic lines consisted often--perhaps by preference--in concluding the strophe with the last melodic line of the *frons*, giving the song the overall form AB AB ...B. In chants of the type under consideration, repetition of melodic lines was not unusual, but it did not necessarily involve the last one. It is not inconceivable that, by changing three of the first four lines, the author of the *Ave regina* adapted Jaufre's *canso* for use in the liturgy. He maintained, however, the repetition of the fourth line as the last line for his chant. For unknown reasons he reduced the melody by combining the fifth and sixth lines of Jaufre's song into one single melody. For the rest, my hypothesis is similar to Brunner's. It is possible that Walther was influenced by both Jaufre's song and its Latin contrafact. Thus, on the basis of data known at present, it is impossible to determine whether Jaufre composed the melody for his most famous song or whether he adapted an existing one.

At one time it was thought that the differences among the surviving versions of a given song were caused by inaccuracy and ignorance on the part of those who copied them from the author's autograph onto the parchment of the surviving manuscripts. Recent research has shown that the troubadours may never have written their melodies down. It is even open to question whether they ever wrote down their poems. A notable exception to this may well have been Guiraut Riquier, who flourished in the second half of the thirteenth century. In general, the songs--text and melody--were transmitted by rote rather than in writing. Not until the middle of the thirteenth century did some afficionados begin to collect songs in writing. (Unfortunately for us, most of those who collected troubadour songs were content with gathering texts only). Accordingly, most of the discrepancies among the multiple versions are probably legitimate and normal variants made during the long period of oral transmission. In addition, those who collected the songs in writing and those who copied them into the extant manuscripts may have made some changes too. This does not mean that the written sources are without errors; it does mean, however, that we can rarely distinguish between a legitimate variant made by a performer or a collector, and an outright scribal error made by a copyist. The former may actually have been sung and should fit into the total character of the song concerned; the latter, on the contrary, is likely to disrupt the natural flow of text or tune.

Since Jaufre's melodies are rather cohesive, it is easier than usual to determine what fits and what does not fit their total character. Jaufre's melodies offer two of those rare occasions in which one can pinpoint a possible error. One of them may well have been made by the person who wrote the tune down upon hearing or from memory; the other may well have been made by the copyist of the extant source. In MS. W, the appearance of E-flat in the last two lines of Song 6 seems out of keeping with the structure of the total song. In MSS. R and X, furthermore, the last line is a note-for-note repetition of lines 2 and 4. It is difficult to determine what, if anything, is actually wrong, but it is quite possible that the scribe of MS. W was confused by knowing more than one version of this melody, including, perhaps, the one for *Ave regina* and/or Walther's song. In any case, a version which resembles closely the 2nd and 3rd melodic lines, like the one given in Figure 1, is more likely to be correct than the one given in the manuscript.[1]

Figure 1. Proposed correction of MS. W's version of the 2nd and 3rd melodic lines of Song 6.

Figure 2. (a) represents the proposed correction of (b), which is the version as found in MS. R.

Figure 3. Transcription of the proposed correction of (a) in Figure 2.

Figure 4. Further correction of the transcription in Figure 3.

The tune of Song 5 may also contain an error. The jump from A to E between the antepenultimate and penultimate syllables of this song is rather strange. In the manuscript it occurs at a change in the placement of the F-clef. Since the shape of this clef (▟) resembles very closely that of a three-note ascending-descending neume (▟ or ▟), it is not inconceivable that the copyist mistook a neume for a clef and thus caused the mentioned anomaly in the melody's flow. The juxtaposition in Figure 2 of (a), what may have been in the copyist's exemplar, and (b), what is actually written in MS. R, shows that such a mistake easily could have occurred. The melody of this hypothetical exemplar--shown in modern notation in Figure 3--is certainly better than what is found in the manuscript, but it is not necessarily the original melody. In order to achieve the most acceptable ending, one would have to lower the pitches for the last two syllables one step, as given in Figure 4.

A final remark concerns Song 3. In MS. M, which has no music, this song appears to have a refrain in that the last verse of each strophe is followed by a two-fold repetition of the rhyme-syllable a. The scribe of this source stands alone, however, in this interpretation. The most important dissenting opinion is given by the music scribe of MS. R, who wrote the notes for the last syllable as one uninterrupted neume, as he did for the last syllables of lines 1 and 3, and as was usual in medieval notation. He thus indicated that the seven notes were to be sung to one, not to three, syllables. Following Jeanroy, Gérold is one of several scholars to accept the version of MS. M as the original one, and to consider the song as having a refrain (Gérold, p. 83). To support his assumption he refers to the song *Pour conforter ma pesance* by Thibaut de Champagne (printed in all versions in van der Werf, *Trouvères Melodien*, II, vol. 12 in *Monumenta Monodica Medii Aevi*, Kassel, 1979, 11-17). This song ends in all sources with a three-fold repetition of the rhyme-syllable e. For Thibaut's song, however, all manuscripts give this repetition. The eight sources with music, moreover, give three separate neumes for the refrain after the neume for the rhyme-word; in some sources the neumes for the refrain are even separated by vertical slashes like the ones appearing often--but not consistently--after the neume for the rhyme-syllable(s). In Thibaut's song, moreover, the three-syllable refrain fits well in the overall form of the poem, as is shown by the following graphic representation of rhyme- and syllable-count:

```
a b    a b    b a C
7'3    7'3    7 7 3
```

Jaufre's song, on the other hand, consists completely of eight-syllable lines. Gennrich published this song twice in two different rhythmizations. On the first occasion he gave the two-fold repetition of the rhyme-syllable as it occurs in MS. M, and split the seven-note neume into three sections of four, two, and one note respectively (*Grundriss*, pp. 243-44); on the second occasion, however, he gave only one repetition of the rhyme-syllable and split the last neume into two sections of four and three notes separated by a rest (*Nachlass*, p. 30). Also, Ismael Fernandez de la Cuesta (de la Cuesta and Laffont, p. 55) divides the last neume of Jaufre's song in two ways. Above the staff, the original neume is split into a group of four and a group of two notes; the last note is missing. On the staff, however, he gives two groups of three notes each--the last note still lacking--with a two-fold repetition of *a* under the latter.

[1]Because of damage to the manuscript, the W version of Song 6 is defective. All but the last clefs and three melodic passages are lacking. The repetition of the first two melodic lines allows restoration of all lacking material excepting the lacuna in the fifth line. More importantly, the placement of the one remaining clef and comparison with the melodies in MSS. R and X reveals the position of all clefs. In MS. W the melody is notated a fifth higher than in the other two sources. In order to facilitate comparison of all versions, its transcription in our synoptic chart is transposed down a fifth.

Bibliography

Aarburg, Ursula. "Probleme um die Melodien des Minnesangs." *Deutschunterricht*, *19* (1967), 98-118. First linked Walther von der Vogelweide's melody to the *Ave regina*.

Aubry, Pierre. *Trouvères et troubadours*. Paris: Alcan, 1910; rpt. Slatkine. Trans. Claude Aveling, New York: Schirmer, 1914; rpt. Cooper Square. Early popularizing introduction.

Beck, Jean-Baptiste. *Anthologie de cent chansons de trouvères et de troubadours des XIIe et XIIIe siècles*. N. p., n. d. Gives text and music (according to the Cangé MS only) of Gautier de Soignies' *Quant oi tentir*, whose refrain refers to *amour lointainne*.

Beck, Jean-Baptiste. *La Musique des troubadours: Etude critique.*
Paris: Laurens, 1928; rpt. AMS, Slatkine. Paris: Stock, 1979.
(See also English translation in Whigham, below). Analyzes
Songs 5 and 6.

_____ and Louise. *Le Manuscrit du roi.* Corpus Cantilenarum
Medii Aevi, I, *2*. 2 vols. Philadelphia: U. of Pennsylvania
Press, 1938; rpt. Broude. Discusses Song 6; attributes anonymous *A l'entrada del tans florit* to Jaufre.

_____, Johann-Baptist. *Die Melodien der Troubadours, nach dem
gesamten handschriftlichen Material zum erstenmal bearbeitet
und herausgegeben.* Strassburg: Trübner, 1908; rpt. AMS.
Introduction to troubadour melodies, with listing of all tunes
then known.

Brunner, Horst, U. Müller and F. V. Spechtler. *Walther von der
Vogelweide: Die gesamte Überlieferung der Texte und Melodien.*
Litterae, 7. Göppingen: Kummerle, 1977. The only extended
discussion of the relationship among the melodies of Jaufre,
Walther, and the *Ave regina*.

_____. "Walthers von der Vogelweide Palästinalied als Kontrafactur." *Zeitschrift für deutsches Altertum,* 92 (1963-64),
195-211. Detailed presentation of Walther's and Jaufre's
melodies in relation to each other.

Bukofzer, Manfred F. "The Fourteenth-Century Motets on St. Edmund." In his *Studies in Medieval and Renaissance Music.*
New York: Norton, 1950. Compares *Ave rex miles Anglorum* to
Ave regina angelorum.

Gennrich, Friedrich. *Der musikalische Nachlass der Troubadours.*
Summa Musicae Medii Aevi, *3-5*. 3 vols. Darmstadt, 1958-65.
Modal transcription of all four Jaufre melodies; listing of
possible contrafacta.

_____. *Grundriss einer Formenlehre des mittelalterlichen Liedes.*
Halle: Niemeyer, 1932. Discusses briefly the four Jaufre melodies; gives modal transcription of two of them, differently
from *Nachlass.*

_____. *Lo Gai Saber: 50 ausgewählte Troubadourlieder: Melodie,
Text, Kommentar, Formenlehre und Glossar.* Musikwissenschaftliche Studien-Bibliothek, *18-19*. Darmstadt, 1959. Transcription of Songs 4 and 6.

_____. "Zur Ursprungsfrage des Minnesangs: Ein literarhistorisch-musikwissenschaftlicher Beitrag." *Deutsche Vierteljahrschrift für Literaturwissenschaft und Geistesgeschichte*, 7 (1929), 187-227. The earliest melodic repetition among the troubadours is in Jaufre.

Gérold, Théodore. *La Musique au moyen âge*. CFMA, 73. Paris: Champion, 1932. Compares stanza-final a a of Song 3 in MS. M to coda in Thibaut de Champagne's *Pour conforter ma pesance*.

Hoppin, Ronald H. *Anthology of Medieval Music*. New York: Norton, 1978. Transcription of Song 4.

_____. *Medieval Music*. New York: Norton, 1978. The most recent discussion available of medieval music.

Husmann, Heinrich. "Das Princip der Silbenzählung im Lied des zentralen Mittelalters." *Die Musikforschung*, 6 (1953), 8-23. First linked Jaufre's melody to Walther von der Vogelweide.

Kippenberg, Burkhard. *Der Rhythmus im Minnesang: Eine Kritik der literar- und musikhistorischen Forschung mit einer Übersicht über die musikalischen Quellen*. Münchener Texte und Untersuchungen zur deutschen Literatur des Mittelalters, 3. Munich: C. H. Beck, 1962. Survey of research on rhythm in medieval song.

La Cuesta, Ismael F. de, Robert Laffont. *Las Cançons dels trobadors*. Toulouse: Institut d'Estudis Occitans, 1979. Transcription of Jaufre's melodies in modern version of medieval notation.

Le Vot, Gérard, Pierre Lusson, and Jacques Roubaud. *La Chanson de "l'amour de loin" de Jaufre Rudel: Essai de lecture rythmique*. Mezura: Cahiers de Poétique Comparée, II, 3. Paris: Publications Orientalistes de France, 1979. A modern version of medieval non-mensural notation, with an original approach to rhythmic analysis.

Maillard, Jean. *Anthologie de chants de troubadours*. Nice: Delrieu, 1967. Transcription in modal rhythm of Song 6.

Monterosso, Raffaello. *Musica e ritmica dei trovatori*. Milano: A. Giuffrè, 1956. Criticism of Beck's varying transcriptions of Song 6.

Posada Amador, Carlos. *Cinco canciones medioevales*. Editorial Cooperativa Interamericana de Compositores, 20. Montevideo: Instituto Interamericano de Musicología, 1943. Spanish version of Song 4, with partly original music.

Restori, Antonio. "Per la storia musicale dei trovatori provenzali: Appunti e note." *Rivista Musicale Italiana*, 2 (1895), 1-22; 3 (1896), 231-60, 407-51. Early study stressing the artificiality of Jaufre's melodies.

Smythe, Barbara. "The Connection between Words and Music in the Songs of the Troubadours." *Modern Language Review*, 3 (1907-08), 329-36. Repetition of melodic phrases in Songs 4 and 6 may have parallels in content.

Tischler, Hans. "Rhythm, Meter, and Melodic Organization in Medieval Songs." *Revue Belge de Musicologie*, 28 (1974), 5-23. Considers the text of Song 6 iambic; gives a trochaic transcription of the music.

Werf, Hendrik van der. *The Chansons of the Troubadours and Trouvères: A Study of the Melodies and Their Relation to the Poems.* Utrecht: Oosthoek, 1972. Introduction to the music of the troubadours; transcribes and discusses Song 6.

Whigham, Peter, ed. *The Music of the Troubadours.* Provençal Series, 1. Santa Barbara: Ross-Erikson, 1979. Section one is a translation by Timothy Wardell of Beck's *Musique*, with an introduction by Alejandro Planchart.

Zerby-Cros, Annie. *Discographie occitane générale: Des troubadours à la "Nouvelle chanson."* Publications du Centre International de Documentation Occitane, Série Catalogues, 3. Béziers: C. I. D. O., Bibliotèca d'Occitania, 1979. Listing of recordings of troubadour music, including many versions of Jaufre's songs.

Discography

Ambe lagrimas e solelh. REV 007. Revolum, 1977. Song 6 sung by Jacmelina.

Cantilènes et chansons de troubadours. HMU 566. Harmonia Mundi, 1969. One stanza of Song 6, after MS. R.

Chansons et motets du XIIIe siècle. ARC 3051 and 14068. DGG Archiv, 1956. First stanza of Song 6, after MS. W.

Le Chant des troubadours. ARN *38503.* Aron, 1979. About four stanzas of Song 6, after MS. W, by the Ensemble Machaut.

French Troubadour Songs of the 12th-13th Centuries. EKL *31.* Elektra, 1955. Songs 3 and 6, with Yves Tessier and Mildred Clary.

Henri Gougaud chante les troubadours. CVR LD *150.* Disques du Cavalier, ca. 1970. Song 6 in modern French translation.

Messe amor a longe. SM *33 05.* Studio Monastères, ca. 1954. A mass by Joseph Samson, based on Song 6. Cf. also a mass (unpublished) based on Song 6 by Robert A. Hall, Jr. of Cornell University.

Monumenta Italiae Musicae: Trouvères & laude. A *00773* R. Philips. Songs 4 and 6 (C. Carbi and R. Monterosso).

Pos de chantar m'es pres talentz. Institut d'Etudes Occitanes. A cassette containing Song 6 read by Pierre Bec, accompanied by Gerard Le Vot.

Troubadours, vol. III. HM *398.* Harmonia Mundi, 1977. *Vida* and extended version of Song 6 by Yves Rouquette and the Clemencic Consortium.

Troubadours, trouvères, et Minnesänger. CEP *104.* Cepedic, 1962. Version of Song 6.

Trouvères et troubadours, Minnesänger et Meistersinger. BAM *103.* Boîte à Musique, 1967. Song 6 by the Ensemble Gaston Soublette.

Trouvères, troubadours, et grégorien. 30M *419.* Studio Monastères, 1956. Songs 5 and 6 (first and last stanzas after MS. W) by Chanterelle del Vasto.

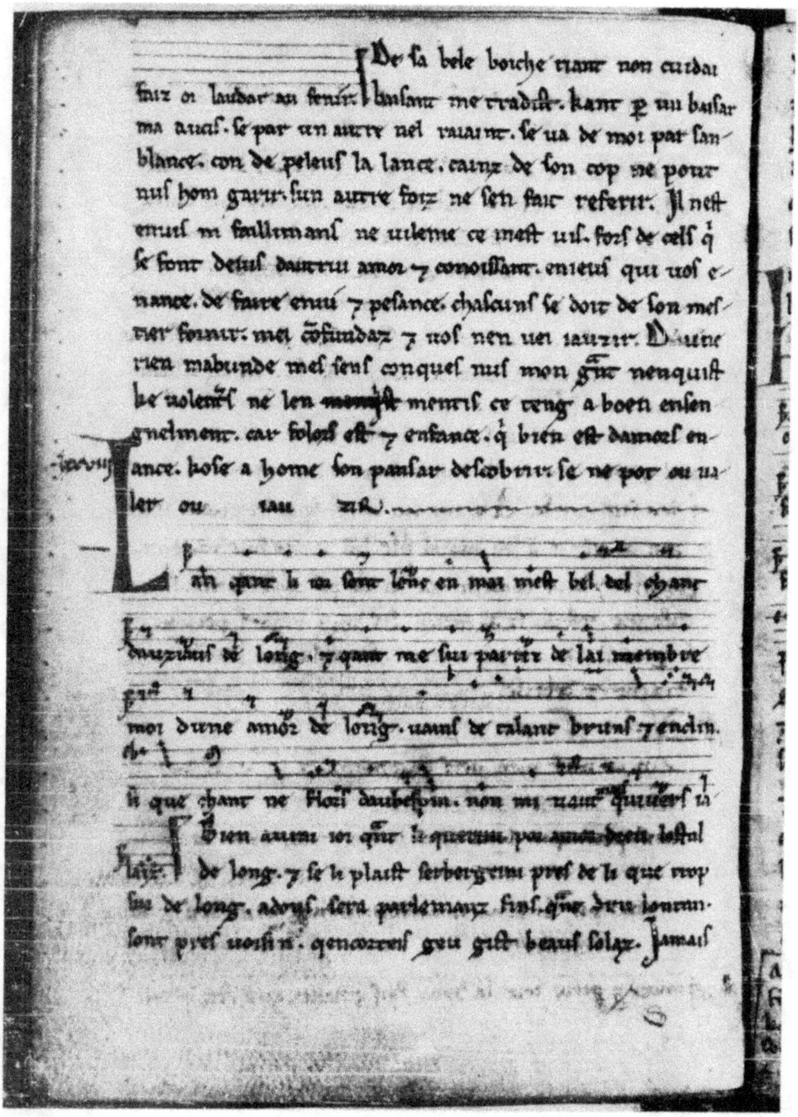

Plate 1. The medieval musical setting for Song 6 in MS. X. Paris, Bibliothèque Nationale, français 20050, folio 81v.

Plate 2. Synoptic chart of lines 1 and 2 of Jaufre's Song 6 (three MSS), Walther von der Vogelweide's *Nu alrest leb'ich mir werde*, and the *Ave regina celorum*.

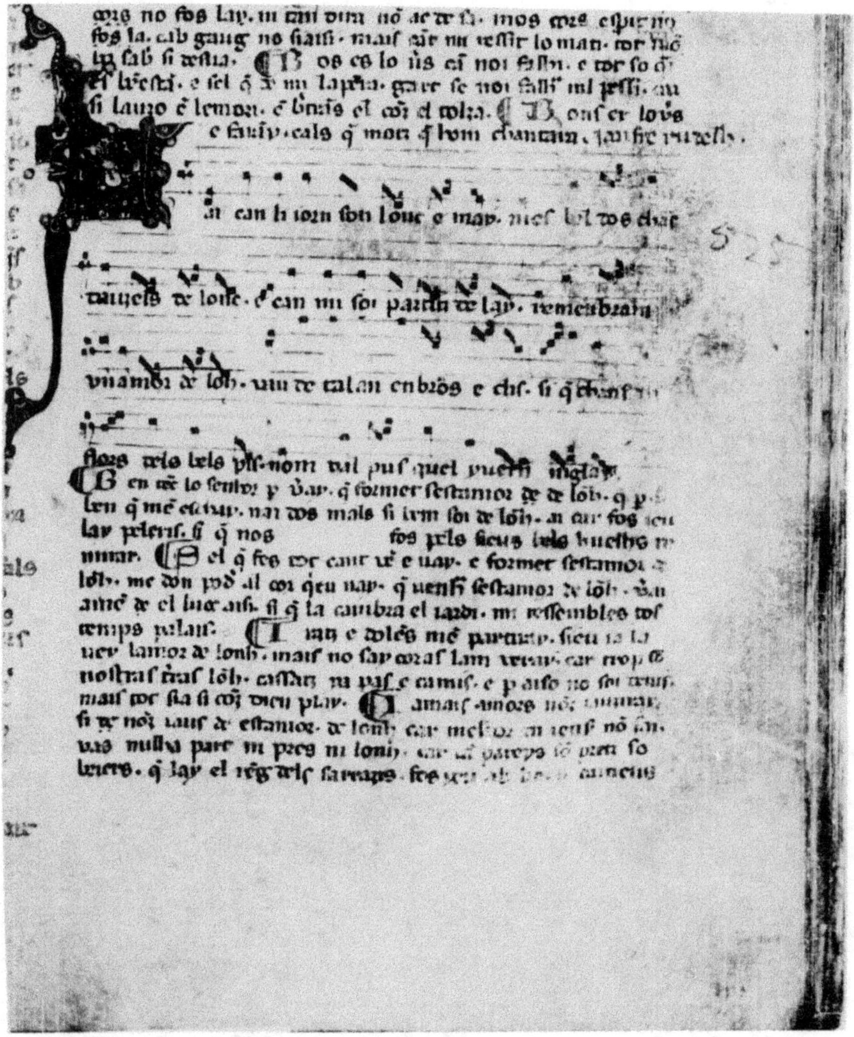

Plate 3. The medieval musical setting for Song 6 in MS. R, Paris, Bibliothèque Nationale, français 22543, folio 63v.

Plate 4. Synoptic chart of lines 3 and 4 of Jaufre's Song 6, Walther von der Vogelweide's *Nu alrest leb'ich mir werde*, and the *Ave regina celorum*.

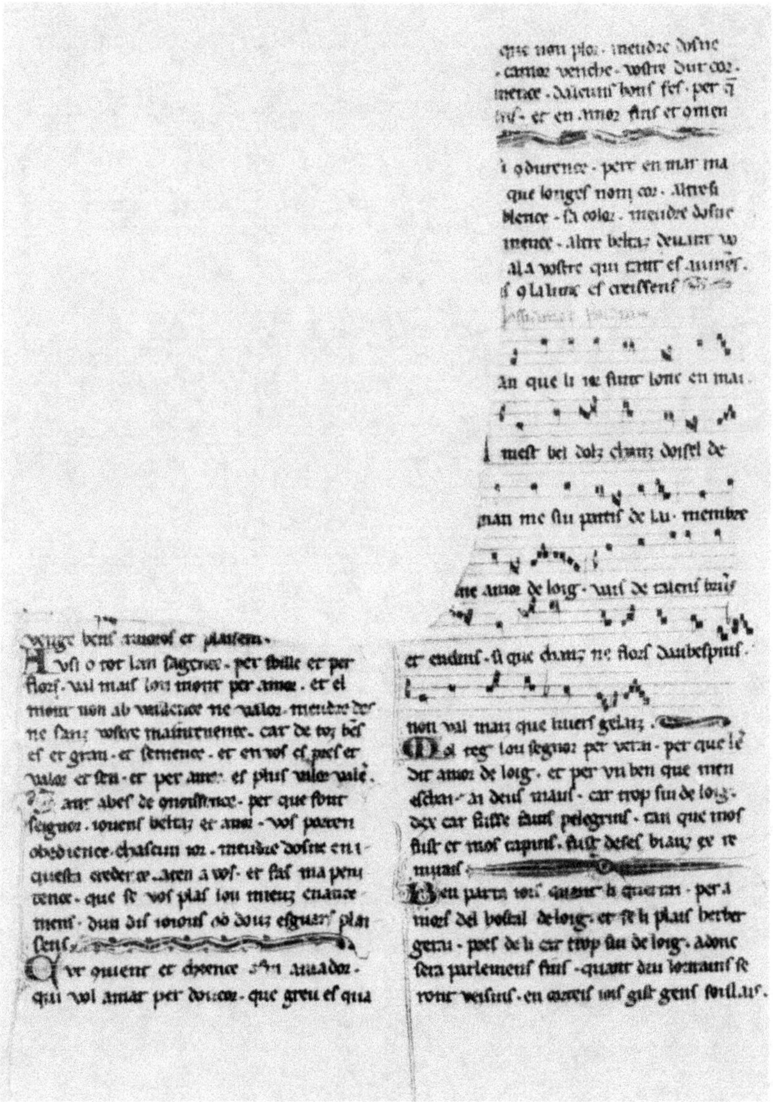

Plate 5. The medieval musical setting for Song 6 in MS. W, Paris, Bibliothèque Nationale, français 844, folio 189v.

Plate 6. Synoptic chart of lines 5 and 6 of Jaufre's Song 6, Walther von der Vogelweide's *Nu alrest leb'ich mir werde*, and line 5 of the *Ave regina celorum*.

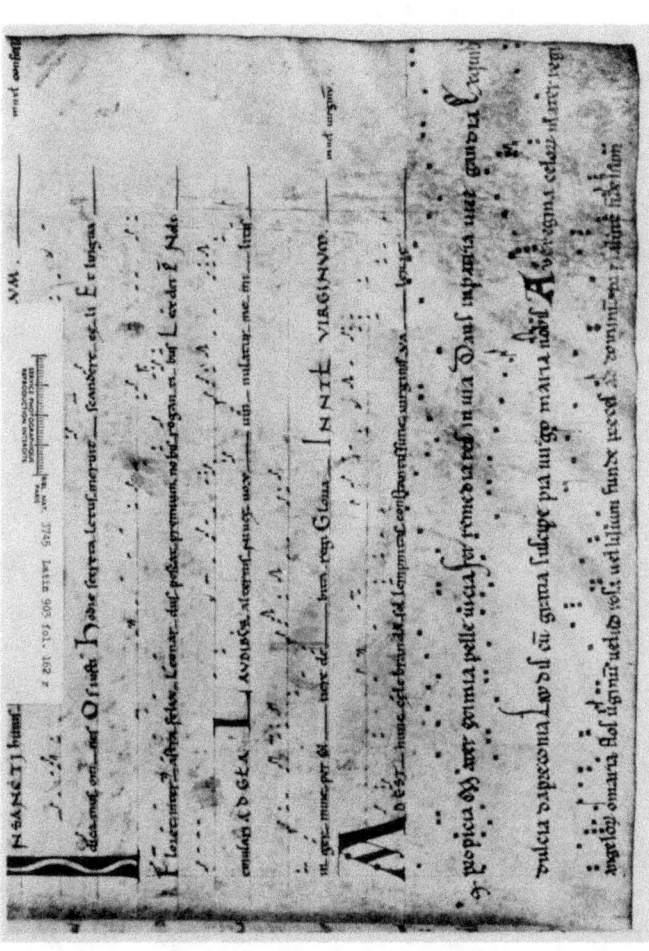

Plate 7. The oldest known version of the *Ave regina angelorum*, a marginal twelfth-century addition to the late eleventh-century gradual of St. Yriex, in southern France. Paris, Bibliothèque Nationale, Latin 903, folio 162r. (Courtesy of the Bibliothèque Nationale)

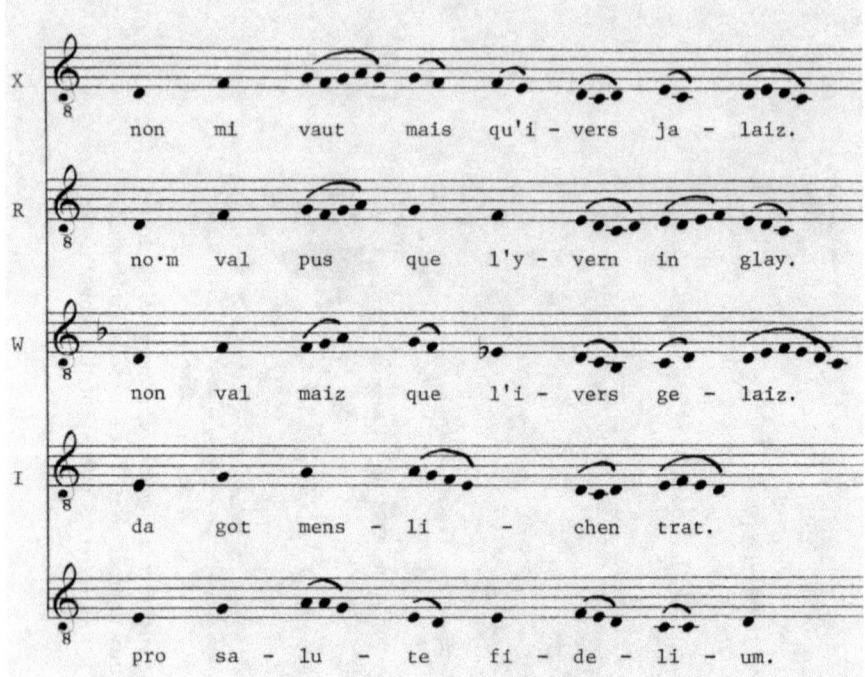

Plate 8. Synoptic chart of line 7 of Jaufre's Song 6, Walther von der Vogelweide's *Nu alrest leb'ich mir werde*, and line 6 of the *Ave regina celorum*.

Plate 9. The medieval musical setting for Song 3 in MS. R, Paris, Bibliothèque Nationale, français 22543, folio 63r.

Plate 10. The melody for Song 3 (MS. R) on a modern staff.

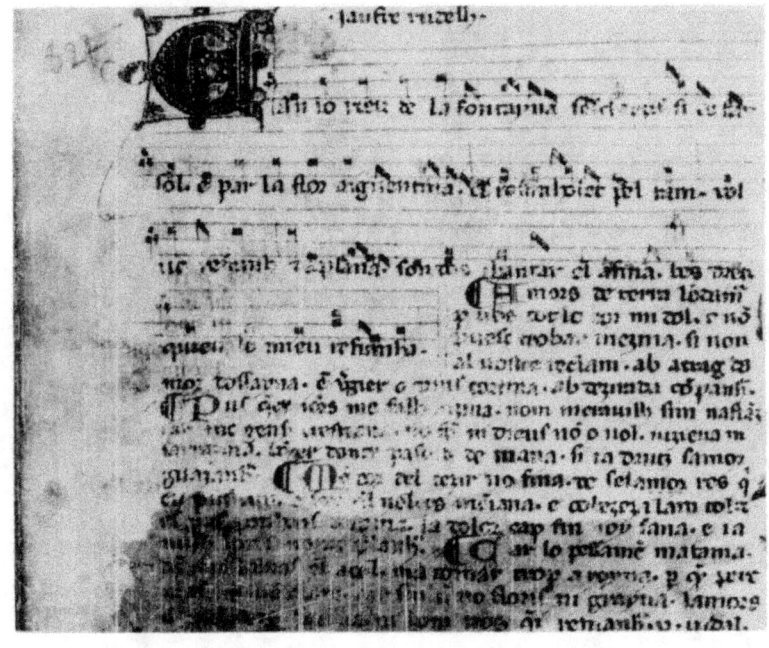

Plate 11. The medieval musical setting for Song 4 in MS. R, Paris, Bibliothèque Nationale, français 22543, folio 63v.

Plate 12. The melody for Song 4 (MS. R) on a modern staff.

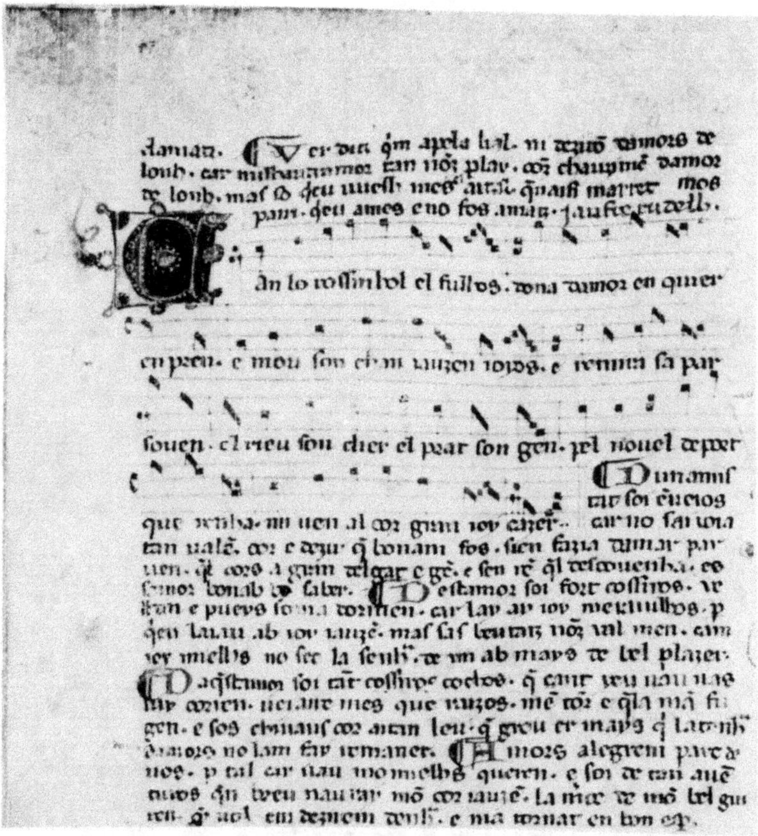

Plate 13. The medieval musical setting for Song 5 in MS. R, Paris, Bibliothèque Nationale, français 22543, folio 63v.

Plate 14. The melody for Song 5 (MS. R) on a modern staff.

For Product Safety Concerns and Information please contact our EU representative GPSR@taylorandfrancis.com
Taylor & Francis Verlag GmbH, Kaufingerstraße 24, 80331 München, Germany

www.ingramcontent.com/pod-product-compliance
Lightning Source LLC
Chambersburg PA
CBHW052112300426
44116CB00010B/1640